Scott, Foresman Social Studies

The photograph on the cover is of a mural
painted by James Yanagisawa and Santi Isrowuthakul
on the wall of an elementary school in Chicago.

Scott, Foresman

SOCIAL STUDIES

Dr. Richard K. Jantz

Associate Professor
Department of Early Childhood—Elementary Education
University of Maryland
College Park, Maryland

Scott, Foresman and Company
Editorial Offices: Glenview, Illinois

Regional Sales Offices: Palo Alto, California •
Tucker, Georgia • Glenview, Illinois •
Oakland, New Jersey • Dallas, Texas

Program Development

Dr. Joan Schreiber
Professor of History
(Social Studies Methods)
Ball State University
Muncie, Indiana

William Stepien
Head, Social Studies Department
School District No. 300
Dundee, Illinois

Dr. Geneva Gay
Associate Professor of Education
Purdue University
West Lafayette, Indiana

Dr. Alan J. Hoffman
Associate Professor of Education
Georgia State University
Atlanta, Georgia

Authors

Dr. Roger M. Berg
Associate Professor
Elementary Education
The University of Nebraska
at Omaha
Omaha, Nebraska

Randee Blair
Teacher—Orrington School
Evanston, Illinois

Dan D'Amelio
Instructional Materials Specialist
Special Education Resource Center
Hartford, Connecticut

Joyce H. Frank
Teacher—Haslett Public Schools
Haslett, Michigan

Dr. Richard K. Jantz
Associate Professor
Department of Early Childhood
Elementary Education
University of Maryland
College Park, Maryland

Judith Medoff
Teacher—Central School
Evanston, Illinois

Dr. Barbara M. Parramore
Associate Professor and Head
Department of Curriculum
and Instruction
School of Education
North Carolina State University
at Raleigh
Raleigh, North Carolina

Dr. Joan Schreiber
Professor of History
(Social Studies Methods)
Ball State University
Muncie, Indiana

Dr. Richard E. Servey
Professor of Elementary Education
San Diego State University
San Diego, California

Priscilla Smith
Teacher—Orrington School
Evanston, Illinois

William Stepien
Head, Social Studies Department
School District No. 300
Dundee, Illinois

Teacher Consultants

Linda Bohan
Teacher—Jordan Acres School
Brunswick, Maine

Barbara Briggs
Teacher—Washington School
Plainfield, New Jersey

Melba F. Coleman
Project Director
Wonders of Work Project
Fifty-Second Street Elementary
School
Los Angeles, California

Althea Cooper
Teacher—Esmond School
Chicago, Illinois

Sue Crow
Teacher—Floydada Public Schools
Floydada, Texas

Marie de Porres, I.H.M.
Teacher—St. Madeline Convent
Ridley Park, Pennsylvania

Frank Espinoza
Teacher—Sierra Vista Elementary
School
Clovis, California

Richard Follett
Environmental Consultant
Public Schools
Santa Rosa, California

Charlie Mae Hutchings
Social Studies Specialist
Chattanooga Public Schools
Chattanooga, Tennessee

Helen Jenkins
Consultant
Nu-Ma-Ku Alternative School
Freeport, New York

Sally Klepack
Teacher—Edgar L. Miller School
Merrillville, Indiana

Alan McAtee
Teacher—Rattlesnake School
Missoula, Montana

Dr. Dorothy J. Mugge
Professor of Early Childhood
Education
Shippensburg State College
Shippensburg, Pennsylvania

Dr. Arthur S. Nichols
Associate Professor of Elementary
Education
California State University
Northridge, California

Barbara Okimoto
Teacher—Burnett Jr. High School
San Jose, California

David Silva
Teacher—Montebello School
Phoenix, Arizona

Marie S. Strickland
Teacher—Donald J. Richey School
Wilmington, Delaware

Serena Westbrook
Teacher—William Paca Elementary
School
Landover, Maryland

Dr. Nancy Wyner
Assistant Professor for Teacher
Education/Social Science
Wheelock College
Boston, Massachusetts

Contents

Charts, Graphs, and Tables

List of Maps and Globes

Scott, Foresman Social Studies

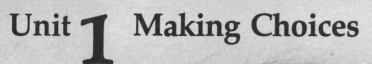

Unit 1 Making Choices

3

Lesson 1 Can It Be Mine?

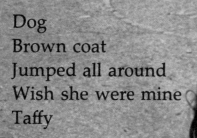

Dog
Brown coat
Jumped all around
Wish she were mine
Taffy

> by Renee

Parrot
Yellow, green
Talked and talked
Hope I can have
Polly

> by Peggy

Rabbit
Fluffy tail
Wiggled his nose
Please make him mine
Fluffy

> by Dan

What kind of pet would you choose? Renee would choose a dog. Dan would choose a rabbit. A parrot would be Peggy's choice.

Choices. You make hundreds of them every day. Some choices are easy to make. These usually are the ones that aren't very important. Should I wear the blue T-shirt or the brown to school today? Should I have toast or cereal for breakfast?

Other choices are harder to make. They are the choices you know you will have to live with. Should I choose a rabbit or dog or a parrot for a pet? Do I want a pet at all knowing how much care it will need? Should I use my time after school to practice for the school play or to earn some money by shoveling snow? Your life is filled with choices.

5

Like Renee and Dan and Peggy, Janis has a choice to make. She must choose between two things she wants very much.

Janis' father promised her a new record album for her birthday. They went to the record store. Janis looked at all the albums. There were hundreds to choose from! She saw many she wanted. Finally, she picked out two.

"Daddy, I can't make up my mind," she said, holding up the two albums. "Can I have both?"

"I promised you one album, Janis," her father said. You'll have to choose. Choose the one you want most."

FOLK A-E

FOLK F-O

7

Choosing means to decide between two or more things or ways of acting. Janis had to choose between two record albums she wanted very much. The boy in the picture is trying to make a choice. He only has ten dollars. The shoes he wants cost fifteen dollars. What choices does he have?

8

Think About It

1. In your own words, tell what "choosing" means.
2. Name some easy choices you have made today.
3. Tell about a difficult choice you have made.

Lesson 2   I Can, but May I?

Janis had trouble making a choice at the record store. She wanted both albums, but her father said, "No!" to that idea.

Janis found that choosing is a difficult thing. To do it well, you have to know the difference between what you can choose, what you cannot choose, and what you may or may not choose.

When you *can* choose something, you *are able to* choose. You *can* choose to let your hair grow longer, but you *can't* choose to have it longer today.

Just because you *can* choose something, however, does not mean you *may* choose it. When you *may* choose something, you *are allowed to* choose. For example, Ivan *can* (is able to) eat dinner under the table. But his parents would, no doubt, say, "Ivan you *may not* (are not allowed to) eat dinner under the table."

What you *may* choose depends on rules.

11

A third-grade class in Maryland studied the differences between *can* and *may*, too. Here is what they wrote about their choices.

I *can* choose:

To be a good friend

 to be a magician when I grow up

my best friend

the person  I want to marry

to learn  about ants

to try to make someone happy

But I *cannot* choose:

what I'll dream
when I am asleep

To be grown up right now

how Tall I'll be

what my name is

where I was born

my brothers and sisters

to hold my breath
for twenty minutes

The third-graders wrote this about what they are allowed to do.

I *may* choose:

When to ride my bike

to play with the baby

to go to the park and swing

what vegetables
I like to eat

which library book To read

To let my hair grow long

a name
for my new puppy

14

But I *may not* choose:

when to Take a bath

a snake for a pet

how much money I have to spend

my Teacher

not to do dishes on my night

to stay home from school
whenever I want

Think About It

1. Name two things you may choose that involve
   —your family.
   —your school and play groups.
   —yourself.
2. Name two things you may not choose that involve
   —your family.
   —your school and play groups.
   —yourself.
3. Why do you think it's important to know what
   you may choose and what you may not?

Lesson 3 How Spider Got a Thin Waist

In West Africa, people tell this story.

 Spider wasn't always as he is today with his
fat head and fat body and thin waist. He was
big and round and his waistline was very fat
indeed. This is how it came to pass that he
looks different today.

One day Spider was walking through the
forest. It was early morning and he noticed a
very pleasant smell. He wrinkled his nose and
sniffed the air. Food! He had almost forgotten.
Today was the festival of the harvest. Every
village in the big forest was preparing a feast.

Spider jumped for joy. His mouth watered. His eyes sparkled, and he smiled brightly. Already he could taste the food.

Now Spider had not done any of the work of preparing for the harvest. He had not planted yams or potatoes. He had not planted rice or gone to sea to catch fish. All day he had played in the sun or slept. But it is not the custom in West Africa to refuse food to anyone who comes to your door. Spider found he could eat very well just by visiting all his friends. In fact, he ate more than they did.

Not far away there were two villages. Today each village would have a great feast.

"How lucky for me!" thought Spider.

But then he was puzzled. Since there were two dinners, he did not know which one he wanted to go to. That is, he did not know which would have the most to eat.

Then Spider got an idea. First, he called his oldest son, Kuma. He took a long rope and tied one end around his waist. The other end he gave to his son.

"Take this rope to the village on the East. When the food is ready, give the rope a hard pull, and I will know it is time for me to come and eat."

Kuma went to the East village and took the end of the rope with him.

18

Then Spider called his youngest son, Kwaku. He took another long rope and tied it around his waist.

"Take this rope to the village on the West. When the food is all cooked, pull very hard on it. Then I will come and have my fill."

So Kwaku went to the West village, carrying the end of the rope with him.

19

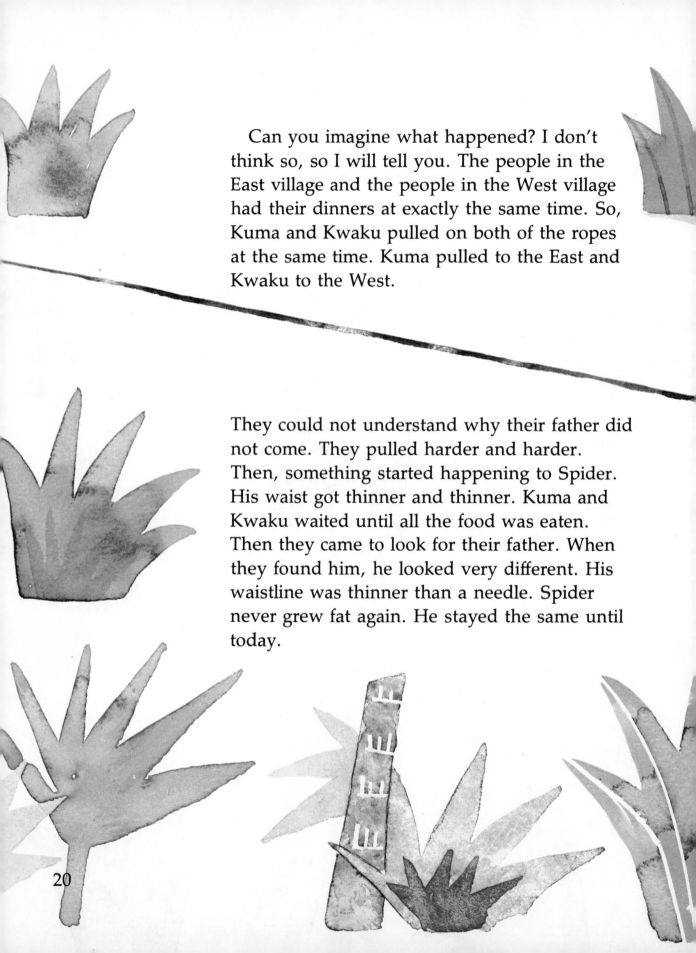

Can you imagine what happened? I don't think so, so I will tell you. The people in the East village and the people in the West village had their dinners at exactly the same time. So, Kuma and Kwaku pulled on both of the ropes at the same time. Kuma pulled to the East and Kwaku to the West.

They could not understand why their father did not come. They pulled harder and harder. Then, something started happening to Spider. His waist got thinner and thinner. Kuma and Kwaku waited until all the food was eaten. Then they came to look for their father. When they found him, he looked very different. His waistline was thinner than a needle. Spider never grew fat again. He stayed the same until today.

21

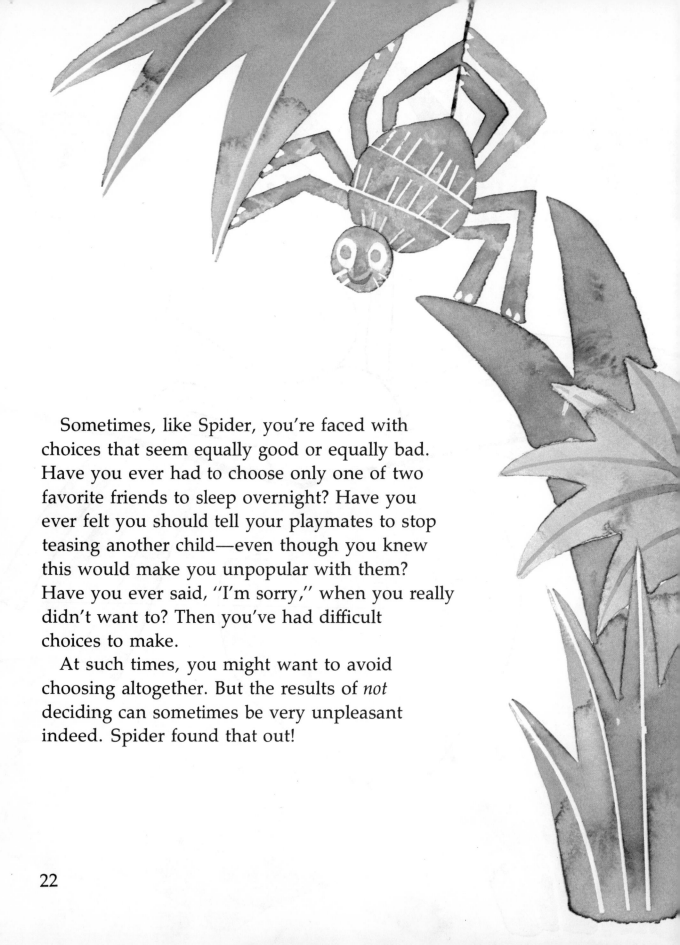

Sometimes, like Spider, you're faced with choices that seem equally good or equally bad. Have you ever had to choose only one of two favorite friends to sleep overnight? Have you ever felt you should tell your playmates to stop teasing another child—even though you knew this would make you unpopular with them? Have you ever said, "I'm sorry," when you really didn't want to? Then you've had difficult choices to make.

At such times, you might want to avoid choosing altogether. But the results of *not* deciding can sometimes be very unpleasant indeed. Spider found that out!

Think About It

1. What choices did Spider have in the story?
2. What did Spider choose?
3. "How Spider Got a Thin Waist" is a West African **folktale.** A folktale is a story that has been handed down by a group of people for **generations.** Folktales can tell a great deal about a people. What does the Spider story tell about life in West Africa?

generation, the people born in the same period. Your parents and their friends belong to one generation; you and your friends to the next.

23

When You Read Social Studies

What is a paragraph? It's a group of sentences. But not all groups of sentences are paragraphs. A paragraph's job is to tell you just one single main idea. If you find more than one main idea in a group of sentences, then it's just that—a group of sentences, not a paragraph.

Look at the two groups of sentences below. Are they paragraphs? What is the main idea in the first group of sentences? Does every sentence talk about how Spider looks? Look at the second group of sentences. Is it a paragraph? What is the main idea?

Spider wasn't always as he is today with his fat head and fat body and thin waist. He was big and round and his waistline was very fat indeed. This is how it came to pass that he looks different today.

Spider wasn't always as he is today with his fat head and fat body and thin waist. Every village in the big forest was preparing a feast. Kwaku went to the West village, carrying the end of the rope with him.

Read the following sentences. Then, on a separate piece of paper, write them in paragraph form. How many paragraphs did you make? What is the main idea of each paragraph?

—Spider had not done any work for the harvest.
—He had not helped plant, and he had not caught fish.
—But that didn't stop him from joining the feast.
—Kuma and Kwaku pulled on both ropes at the same time.
—They could not understand why their father did not come.
—When they finally found their father, he looked very different.

What Do You Know?

Words to Know

Match the words on the left with the correct meanings on the right. Write your answers on another sheet of paper.

1. folktale
2. choose
3. choice
4. generation

a. person or thing chosen
b. a story handed down by a group of people from one generation to another
c. to pick out something
d. the people born in the same time period

Ideas to Know

Some of the sentences below are true and some are not. Number a paper from 1 to 5. Write "yes" next to the number if the statement is true; write "no" if the statement is not true.

1. Deciding whether or not to do something is making a choice.
2. When someone decides something for you, you have made a choice.
3. There are some things you can't choose.
4. Some choices are difficult to make.
5. What you may choose depends on rules.

Using What You Know

Read the cartoon below. Tell if Charlie Brown *can* throw a snowball at Lucy. *May* Charlie Brown throw a snowball at Lucy? Why or why not?

27

Unit 2 How You Decide

28

Lesson 1 What Can You Do?

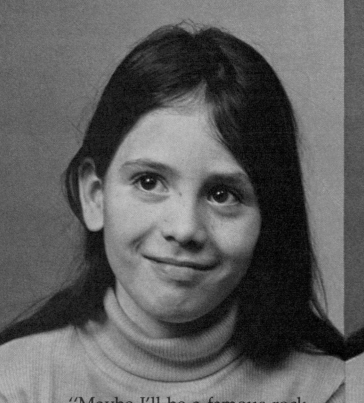

"Maybe I'll be a famous rock star when I grow up. I love to play guitar."

"On second thought, maybe I won't be a rock star. I *hate* getting up in front of crowds."

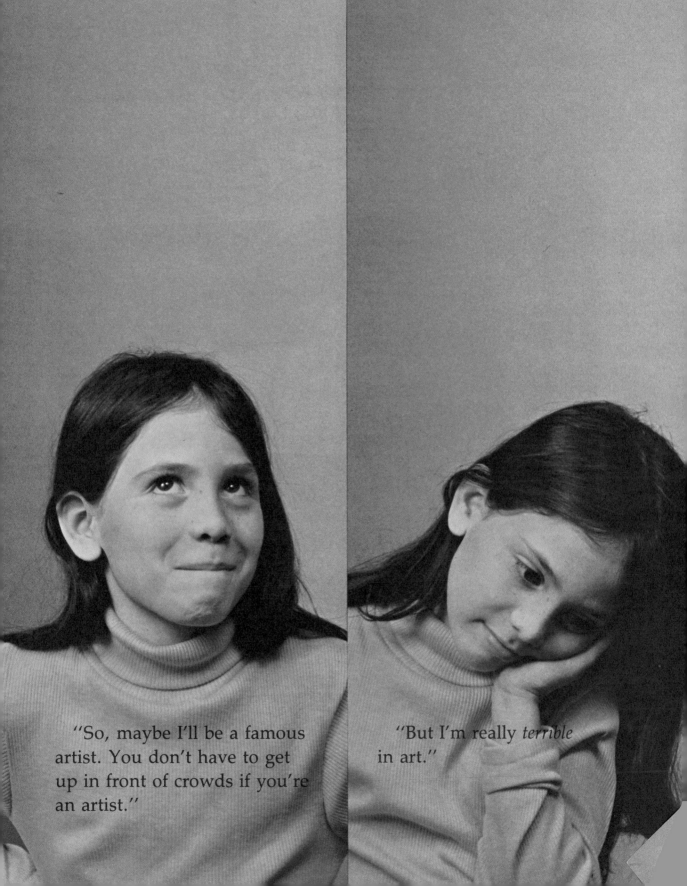

"So, maybe I'll be a famous artist. You don't have to get up in front of crowds if you're an artist."

"But I'm really *terrible* in art."

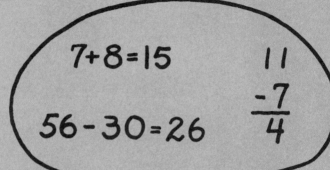

"What I *am* good at is math. There are *lots* of things you can be if you're good in math!"

32

Everyone has some things he or she can do well. Some people are good at performing for groups. Some are good in math; some in art. Some are good at telling two bugs apart. We call the things people are good at their **abilities.**

Your abilities affect your choices. Suppose, for example, that you had your choice of playing volleyball or football. And suppose you *never* score at volleyball, but you're *great* at football. Which would you choose to play? Everyone likes to **succeed**. So most people would choose to do the things they can do well.

succeed, do well; have success.

Eight Is Great!

Eight is Great!
I can do so many things now
I couldn't do at Six.

Like tell time.

And whistle.

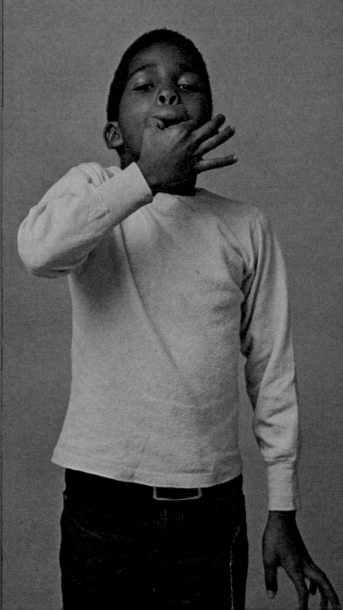

34

And swim.
(I passed the test.)

And that's not including
The thing I do best!

Your abilities can change. Sometimes learning can change your abilities. You can learn to swim or tell time.

You change as you grow. Sometimes these changes affect your abilities. Probably the boy on page 34 couldn't whistle when he was six because too many of his teeth were out!

Sometimes lots of work can change your abilities. Suppose you're a terrible batter. You're the last one picked when your playmates are choosing teams. But suppose your older brother or sister worked with you on your batting every night. With lots of practice, you might become a good batter.

When your abilities change—for whatever reason—so do your choices. That's why it's always good to try lots of different things. You never know when you'll discover something new you can do.

Maybe you'll find you can't do some new things well. But you might find things you have *fun* doing!

Think About It
1. What are abilities?
2. List some of your abilities.
3. How can abilities change?

39

What can you be if

You might be a meteorologist and try to say
what the weather will be . . .

$$\begin{array}{r} 21 \\ 43 \\ +58 \\ \hline 128 \end{array}$$

or a buyer of food for restaurants . . .

you're good at math?

or a teller in a bank . . .

or a chef . . .

or a chemical engineer . . .

or an accountant . . .

There are hundreds of jobs a person good at math can do. Can you name some others?

Lesson 2   Hop, Hop, and Away!

All the frogs in the big pond in the woods spent the whole day hopping from one lily pad to the next. All of them except one, that is. Herman sat on the same lily pad all day long and watched the other frogs hop by.

"Come on, Herman," the other frogs would call. "We're going to have a contest. Whoever makes the biggest jump from one lily pad to another wins."

"I'd like to," Herman would say sadly. "But I know I wouldn't make it."

Soon the other frogs stopped asking him. It wasn't as if Herman hadn't tried to learn how to hop from pad to pad like the other frogs. He tried many times. But each time he tried, "Kerplunk!" He ended up in the water and someone would have to pull him out. (It was *very* embarrassing.) So after a while he just sat.

One day, after Herman had been sitting on his lily pad for quite some time, a Wise Old Frog happened to hop by. The Wise Old Frog watched Herman for a while and then he asked, "Why don't you ever move, son?"

Herman sighed and told the Wise Old Frog the whole story.

"So I guess I'm going to spend the rest of my days on the same old lily pad," Herman sighed.

"Nonsense!" said the Wise Old Frog. "You were much younger when you last tried to hop. Your legs have no doubt grown since then. Try again!"

"Oh, I thought of that," Herman said shaking his head. "But I haven't used my muscles in so long I *know* I wouldn't make it."

45

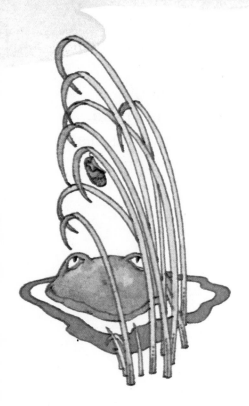

The Wise Old Frog thought a minute. Then he said, "Had a case just like yours in my own family once. Fella had a terrible case of Hopping Fright. Sat on the same lily pad for months before he got up the courage to hop. Did just fine, though, when he tried."

"Really?" Herman said hopefully.

"The honest truth," the Wise Old Frog said, trying to give Herman confidence. The Wise Old Frog believed Herman could make it. He knew that if only Herman believed it too he would be able to hop to the next lily pad.

"Come on, give it a try," Wise Old Frog urged. "There's a big beautiful pond out there. You want to see it, don't you?"

"OK. I-I-I'll try," Herman said.

Herman closed his eyes tight so he could **concentrate**. Then he took a deep breath and pushed off the lily pad with all his might. And "Smack!" He landed right in the middle of the pad next to him. The Wise Old Frog cheered.

concentrate, pay close attention.

"I did it! I did it!" Herman shouted. "How wonderful it is to hop. Thank you Wise Old Frog for giving me the confidence to try!"

And Herman hopped away across the big pond.

Herman's experiences told him that he couldn't hop from lily pad to lily pad like the other frogs. So he chose to stay on the same old lily pad even when he had the ability to hop to the next. Herman's experiences influenced his choices.

Think About It

1. When Herman met Wise Old Frog did he have the ability to hop to the next lily pad? What stopped him?

2. What are experiences? How can they affect your choices?

3. Have you ever had an experience like Herman's when you thought you couldn't do something you really could do?

49

When You Read Social Studies

You don't always have a dictionary handy when you read. How can you find out the meanings of words you don't know? Sometimes the words and sentences around unfamiliar words give clues to their meaning. To get an idea of how this works, complete the sentences below. Then, tell how the other words in each sentence helped you think of the missing word.

Bill gave the kitten
some _____ to drink.
(What might a kitten drink?)

Jackie heard the _____
singing in the tree.
(What might sing in a tree?)

Your mind works the same way when filling in the "blank" created in a sentence by an unfamiliar word. Read the following paragraphs from "Hop, Hop, and Away." See if you can tell the meaning of the word "confidence" from the other sentences in the paragraphs.

"The honest truth," the Wise Old Frog said, trying to give Herman confidence. The Wise Old Frog believed Herman could make it. He knew that if only Herman believed it too he would be able to hop to the next lily pad.

"I did it! I did it!" Herman shouted. "How wonderful it is to hop. Thank you Wise Old Frog for giving me the confidence to try!"

Lesson 3 Yellow Day, Gray

Bad Day
Yesterday it was great,
A yellow day. It made my feet run
And my arms flap
And my voice sing

(Oh sing aloud
If sing you can!)

And I was alive.
Really alive.

52

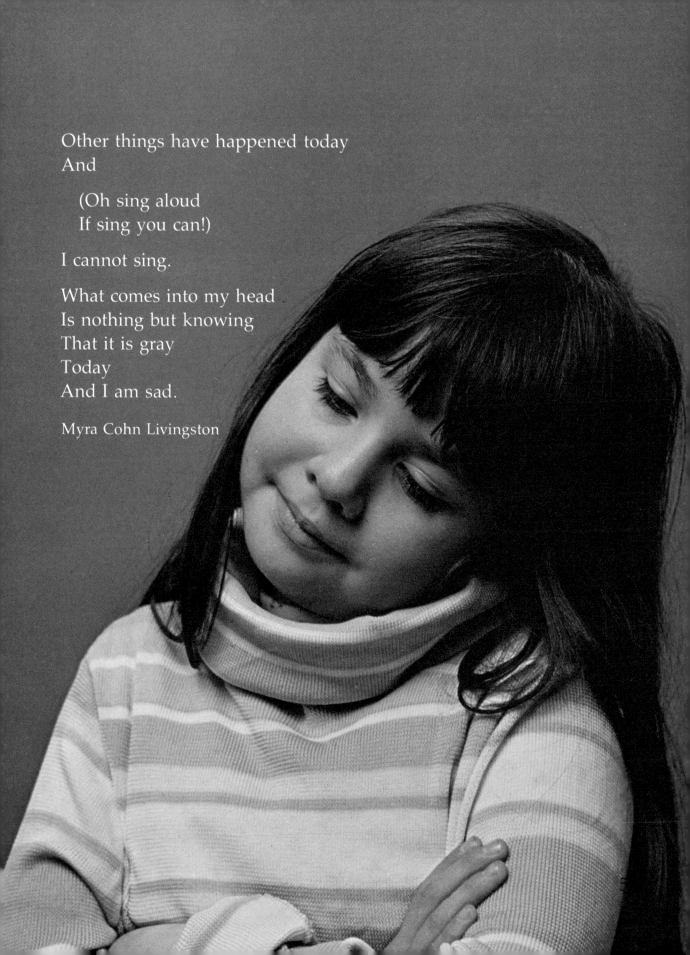

Other things have happened today
And

   (Oh sing aloud
   If sing you can!)

I cannot sing.

What comes into my head
Is nothing but knowing
That it is gray
Today
And I am sad.

Myra Cohn Livingston

Which would you choose to do on a "yellow day" when you felt just great? Take a run down your favorite hill? Help your sister teach your dog some tricks? Sit quietly in your room? Which would you choose to do on a "gray day" when you felt sad? How do your feelings affect your choices?

Have you ever heard someone say something like this? "I feel like playing some ball with my friends." Or, "I feel like talking to Granddad." Or "I don't know why I started an argument with Peter. I guess I'm just in a bad **mood** today."

Your moods or feelings affect your choices. When your mood changes, so do your choices.

Think About It

1. What word means the same as feelings?
2. Have you ever got up feeling good, made great plans for the day, and then had something happen to change your mood completely? Tell about it. How did your mood change affect your plans?
3. Have you ever got up feeling grouchy and then had something happen to make you feel happy? How did it affect your plans?

mood, state of mind or feeling.

Lesson 4   Good News

56

"Jeff, I've got two tickets for the baseball game this Saturday," Sidney said. "Do you want to come?"

Jeff didn't need any time to think about it. "Do I? I haven't been to a game yet this season."

"Good!" said Sidney. "Then it's all set! My mother and I will pick you up at one o'clock."

At supper, Jeff told his parents his good news. "But that's the day Papa Franklin is coming to visit. He'll be very disappointed if he doesn't get to see you," his father said.

In his excitement over the baseball game, Jeff had forgotten about Papa Franklin's visit. Jeff thought a minute. Then he said, "Papa Franklin would want me to go to the game, I think. He always wants me to have a good time."

"Well, I think he'll be disappointed," Jeff's mother said. "But it's up to you to decide what you should do."

"I've decided to go to the game," Jeff said.

That night, Jeff thought about Papa Franklin. He thought about how his grandfather always listened to him carefully—as if Jeff had really important things to say. He thought about how his grandfather fixed his bike on his last visit (after Dad said it couldn't be fixed). And he remembered all the great stories his grandfather told him about what it was like when he was growing up down South.

The next morning, Jeff said to his father, "Do you *really* think Papa Franklin will feel bad if I'm not here?"

"Yes, Jeff. I do."

"Then I guess I won't go to the game," Jeff said sadly.

"There will be other games," his father said.

That Saturday, when Jeff saw Papa Franklin coming up the walk, he was glad he made the choice he did.

People choose what they think is important. What did Jeff think was important? How did this affect his choices?

How do we choose? Many things affect our choices. Our abilities affect our choices. We often choose to do what we can do well, what we've experienced success doing. If we choose to do only the things we can do well, however, we limit our choices and miss out on a lot of fun. Also, learning, physical changes, hard work, and many other things can change our abilities.

Our moods also affect our choices. So do the things we think are important.

Think About It
1. Why do you think Jeff made the choice he did?
2. What do you think you would have done in Jeff's place?
3. List some things that affect choices.
4. Tell *how* they affect choices.

What Do You Know?

Words to Know

Match the words on the left with the correct meanings on the right. Write your answers on another sheet of paper.

1. ability   **a.** having an effect on another person
2. confidence   **b.** something that happens to you
3. experience   **c.** belief in your abilities
4. influence   **d.** being able to do something

Ideas to Know

Some of the sentences below are true and some are not. Number a paper from 1 to 6. Write "yes" next to the number if that statement is true; write "no" if it's not true.

1. Everyone is good in math.
2. Most people choose to do things that they can *not* do well.
3. Your abilities can change.
4. An experience is something to eat.
5. Your feelings can affect your choices.

Using What You Know

We choose different things for different reasons. Most of the time, we don't think about *why* we choose things. To find out how *you* choose, try this. Make a list of 10 things you would choose to do. Then:

1. If there are things on your list that you can do well, or with a great deal of **ability,** write **A** next to them. (You can have more than one letter next to each item on your list.)
2. If you have had good or pleasant **experiences** doing any of the things on your list, write **E** next to them.
3. If there are things on your list that you would choose to do if you are in a **mood** to be **outdoors,** write **MO** next to those. Write **MI** next to those you choose when you are in a **mood** to be **indoors.**
4. If there are any things on your list you would choose if you are in the **mood** to be with other **people,** write **MP** next to them. If there are any you would choose if you're in the **mood** to be **alone,** write **MA** next to them.

Now look over your list carefully. Which letters do you have the most of? Do you have a lot of As? Then you like to do what you're good at. And so on.

Unit **3** People Affect You

Lesson 1   Getting the Message

How do you think the children in the picture are influencing the boy's choice? Have your friends ever influenced you? Have you ever said: "Why can't I have a ten-speed bicycle like everyone else?" Or, "Why can't I camp out all night? Everybody else can."

If you have, then you know that other people can influence your choices.

Sometimes people influence you by things they say. Other times people can influence you without using words at all. They tell you things just by the looks on their faces or by the positions of their bodies. These are **messages** they send out to tell you what they're thinking or feeling.

Look at these three children. Can you "read" the messages they're sending out? What are they thinking and feeling? How would you **respond** to each of them? That is, what would you say or how would you act in answer to their messages?

People can influence you by the things they say and the ways they act. Sometimes, though, people's words and actions don't tell exactly how they feel.

Suppose, for example, that it's your birthday and a friend is treating you to a pizza. When it's time to give your order, you say, "How about sausage?" just as he says, "Let's get mushroom." Suppose that then he says, "Sausage is all right with me, if that's what you want."

What do you think he really meant? It might have been: "I don't really like sausage pizza very much, but I like you. I want this pizza to be something you enjoy."

It's important to think about what people really mean. It helps you understand how to respond to them. Study the cartoon on these pages. What would have happened if Julie hadn't understood Carol's real feelings?

Think About It

1. How have others influenced your choices?
2. How can people influence you without using words?
3. Why is it important to think about what people are really thinking and feeling?
4. How might Julie have acted if Carol had said what she really felt?

MAYBE I SHOULDN'T LET ANYONE RIDE IT YET. I JUST GOT IT.

DO YOU WANT TO TAKE A RIDE ON IT? YOU'VE GOT TO BE CAREFUL.

CAROL LOOKS PRETTY WORRIED. MAYBE I'D BETTER WAIT UNTIL SHE'S HAD IT AWHILE.

NO, THAT'S O.K. I'LL RIDE IT SOME OTHER TIME.

CONSUMER CONCERNS

Why Do You Buy?

Advertisements can influence your choices. Look at the advertisement below. Then try to answer the questions.

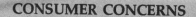

"Be like world champion runner, Karen Cannon. Start your day with PEP POPS! Get some TODAY!"

pep POPS

1. How is the ad trying to influence your choice of breakfast cereals?
2. What does the ad suggest will happen if you eat PEP POPS?

72

3. What group of people is the ad talking to?
4. Give some reasons why people might buy PEP POPS after seeing this ad.
5. Tell about an ad that has influenced you.

73

Lesson 2   Learning to Choose

People begin to influence how you think and act very early in life—even before you can talk or understand when others talk to you. Usually, the members of your family are the first to influence you. They teach you things in the first months of life that can affect your behavior for many years to come.

For example, if you were often hugged and held close as a small baby, you probably learned to respond in the same way to others as you grew older. If your family rushed to answer your cries, you learned trust. Your family's behavior taught you—"When I'm hungry or frightened, someone always comes to help me."

As you grow older, your family begins to set down rules for you to follow. They tell you in words or actions how they think you should behave. They hope that these rules will help you make choices about how to act that will keep you safe, make you happy, and help you get along with others.

Sometimes children find it hard to follow all the rules their families make. Take Rosamund, for example. Sometimes she's *very* good. Sometimes she behaves otherwise. Do you ever behave like Rosamund? Read the poem and find out.

Two People

Two people live in Rosamund,
    And one is very nice;
The other is devoted
    To every kind of vice—

To walking where the puddles are,
    And eating far too quick,
And saying words she shouldn't know,
    And wanting spoons to lick.

Two people live in Rosamund,
    And one (I say it twice)
Is very nice *and* very good:
    The other's only nice.

Rosamund's family probably gave her some rules to guide her behavior. Match the things Rosamund liked to do with the reasons her family might have given for not doing them.

wanting spoons to lick

walking in puddles

eating far too quickly

saying words she shouldn't know

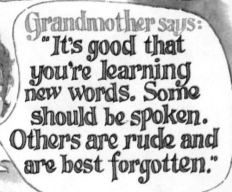

Mother says: "Rosamund, food tastes better when you eat it slowly. When you eat too fast, your stomach doesn't know what your throat just swallowed."

Big Brother says: "If spoons were to lick, Rosamund, they'd be lollipops."

Grandmother says: "It's good that you're learning new words. Some should be spoken. Others are rude and are best forgotten."

Father says: "Rosamund, when you walk in puddles, your shoes get wet and stay wet the whole day. You'd feel much better in dry shoes."

Think About It

1. A rule usually is made for a reason. List some rules your family has made and the reasons why you think they were made.
2. How many family rules are made to keep you safe and healthy or to help you get along with others?
3. How does your behavior at school and play show what you have learned at home?

Lesson 3   I Want a Horse!

Most people live in a **community** of one kind or another. A community can be any size, large or small. It can be in or near a city or far from one. A community is made up of people who live and work near each other in a certain place.

A person who lives in a community in our country often belongs to many groups. For example, you belong to a family, school, and play group. You may also belong to a church group and a club or two.

Each of these groups can influence your choices. Because so many people and groups influence your choices, making a decision in a community is often difficult.

Let's see how difficult making choices in a community can be. Suppose a child who lives in a city community wants a horse. Here are some people and groups that might influence his or her choice.

People watching a Fourth of July parade in Evanston, Illinois.

79

I decided I wanted a horse.

How would we pay for it?
Who would take care of it?
Where would we keep it?
The neighbors wouldn't like it.

I'll help you take care of it if I can ride it sometimes.

You'd better ask your mom and dad.

So I talked to my family.

My friends thought it was a GREAT idea.

So I talked to some neighbors.

So I talked to Officer Perez.

Think About It

1. Name the groups Molly had to talk with about her decision to get a horse.
2. What are some problems a horse might cause in Molly's community?
3. Why do you think the city government had made a law against keeping horses in backyards?
4. What are some good things about living in a community?
5. What are some bad things?

Lesson 4   The Amish

If you came to the community of Belleville, Pennsylvania, on a summer Saturday, you would see a sight you'd long remember. On the streets, the usual rows of parked cars line the curbs. But many horses stamp their feet nearby, gently moving the black buggies they're hitched to.

Many people in Belleville dress just as people in your town, but some do not. Those who don't usually wear dark clothes. The men and boys wear straw hats or felt hats with wide brims. Girls and women wear caps, shawls, and apron-covered dresses.

Who are these people who have come to town for the day? They are the Amish.

84

The Amish are groups of people who believe that the Bible tells them to keep apart from those who are not Amish. For this reason, they have chosen to start their own communities and their own schools. Many Amish communities are found in Ohio, Indiana, and Pennsylvania.

The Amish believe in depending on each other in their communities. If one neighbor needs help building a barn, others gladly help. Painting a kitchen or sawing wood or sewing a quilt often brings neighbors together to help each other.

Most of the Amish are farmers. This is because they believe that working the land brings them closer to God. Farming also keeps families together and their **beliefs** strong. The Amish feel that working in towns and cities among people who do not believe as they do would weaken these ties.

The Amish believe in a life of hard work without things to make life easier. So Amish people don't own things like tractors, farm machines, or automobiles.

belief, an idea a person holds to be true.

85

To keep their beliefs strong, the Amish have developed a set of rules to live by. Some of these rules simply allow the Amish to appear different from other Americans, to send out a message that says, "I am Amish. I believe differently from you." Other rules help the Amish stay apart from other people.

Here are a few rules most Amish try to follow.

They must wear dark clothes.

Women must wear caps and shawls in public.

Women must wear aprons at all times.

Men and boys must wear hats at all times unless in a house, at school, or at a Sunday meeting.

Married men must grow beards, but must shave their mustaches.

They must help Amish people in need.

They must use no electricity from an electric company.

They must have no cars, televisions, or telephones.

They may not marry anyone who does not believe in the Amish religion.

They must **shun** those who break the rules of the Amish.

shun, keep away from.

Amish children don't always have the same choices as you. They can't choose to watch television programs. They can't choose to talk to a friend on the telephone. But like you, their choices are affected by their abilities, experiences, feelings, and values. They are influenced by their family members and by their groups, just as you are. The choices Amish children make are influenced by the beliefs of their community. Your choices are influenced by your community, too.

Think About It

1. How are your choices influenced by your community?
2. What kinds of choices do Amish children make that are the same as yours?
3. What kinds of choices are different from yours?
4. How does the Amish community try to set itself apart from others? For what reasons?

When You Read Social Studies

Who are the Amish? How much do you know about them? The lesson you just read told you some things. For example, you know about some of their beliefs and some of their rules. You know that many of the Amish are farmers. You know how they dress.

But the lesson didn't cover everything. No lesson could in eight pages. Were you left with any questions? Did you wonder, for example, what Amish children do in their free time? What games they play? What holidays they celebrate?

If you did have questions like these, you don't need to keep wondering. You can answer a lot of the questions yourself by checking other books. For example, if you wanted to find out more about growing up as an Amish boy or girl, you might enjoy a book called *Shoo-Fly Girl* by Lois Lenski. Or, to learn more about Amish people and their ways, you could read *Amish Wedding* by Florence W. Rowland.

How can you find these books? You might begin by looking in the card file in your school's library. For every book in the library, there is a card filled out. Each card includes the subject, title, and author of the book. The cards are filed alphabetically by title, author, and subject. This means that you can find a book by looking under the subject you're interested in, such as "Amish," by the title of the book, *Shoo-Fly Girl,* or by the author, Lois Lenski.

The cards in the file also have on them numbers, letters, or both. These tell you where the books can be found in the library. If you're a good library detective, you might be able to find the book yourself. Libraries usually have signs showing where all the books in the series of numbers and letters are located.

But if you have trouble finding what you're looking for, here's a sure rule to follow: ask your librarian.

What Do You Know?

Words to Know

Match the words on the left with the correct meanings on the right.

1. respond
2. belief
3. community
4. message

a. groups of people who live and work near each other and who depend on each other

b. speak or act in answer to someone else's words or actions

c. an idea that a person or group holds to be true

d. words or actions sent from one person to another

Ideas to Know

Make a list of some groups in your community that influence your choices. The pictures below will give you some ideas. Then write a sentence telling how each group influences your choices.

Using What You Know

Look at the picture below. That's Eric. What has he learned to do? What other things might he need to know? Who could teach him?

Unit 4 The World Around You

95

Lesson 1   Sand Castles and Tall Buildings

A newspaper reporter asked some children in Chicago, Illinois: "How would you describe your city to a stranger?" This is what the children said.

"They have fireworks every year. My family comes out to the lake to look at them. You can go out to the beach every day. Chicago has the tallest building in the world. They can go to the top of it and look out on the city. They can see the different neighborhoods and all the people."

Vito Rotindi
Student, Near North Side

"It is a nice place to live in. People are friendly. You can do stuff like paint and art and play. The weather is kind of cool. There are big buildings. They are nice to look at. You can see animals at the zoo. All different kinds of people live here. Some are nice. (Some aren't so nice.)"

Sammy Cuellar
Student, South Side

96

"There is sand on the beach and water you can swim in. You can lay in the sun and stuff. You could play and build sand castles and stuff. You can see some of the city too when you look across the street. There are a lot of nice people. . . ."

Gina Guzzo
Student, Northwest Side

"It gets cold in the winter and the fall. It gets warm in the spring and summer. . . .You can see bears and tigers and monkeys in the zoo too. There are a lot of fun things to see and do here."

Diana Southern
Student, Northwest Side

97

This is the beach where the children swim. The tall buildings in the picture are the ones the children can see when they look across the street.

Chicago is a very big city. Almost seven million people live there. The children can see only a few of the tallest buildings from the beach. Other buildings extend on for many more miles. They are the apartment and office buildings, houses, factories, and stores where the people of Chicago live and work.

98

This picture was taken from the John
Hancock building, one of the tallest in Chicago.
It shows a little more of the city than the picture
on pages 98 and 99. See all the buildings. The
beach where the children swim is at right
below.

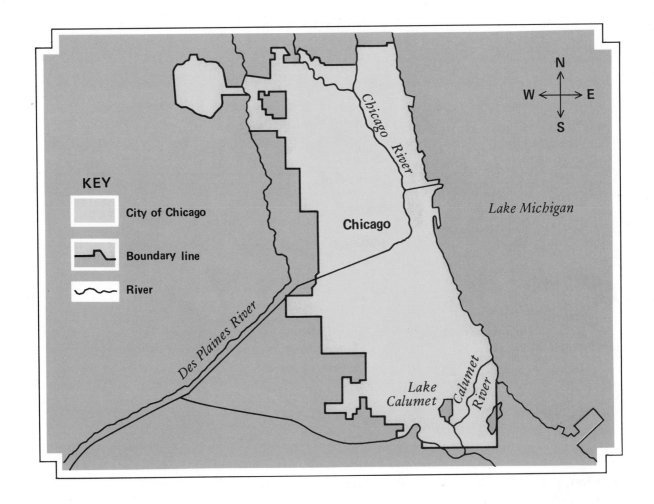

The map above gives an even better idea of how Chicago looks. The yellow area shows the shape of the city. Trace the line that shows where Chicago ends with your finger. This line is called a **boundary.** Sometimes a river may form a boundary. Find some places on the map where rivers form part of Chicago's boundary.

Find the lake where the children swim. What is its name? Is this lake east or west of the city? Where is the beach? Is it on the east or west side of the city?

101

location, place or
position of something.

The **location** of Chicago has a lot to do with
what the children can do there. Because
Chicago is located on Lake Michigan, the
children can choose to go swimming in the lake
and to build sand castles on the beach.

Where is your community located? Is it near
mountains? On an ocean? By a river? How do
you think your community's location will affect
your choices?

Think About It
1. How would you describe your community?
2. Tell how your community's location affects
   what you can do there.
3. Locate your community on a map.

When You Read Social Studies

Chicago is a very large city. In fact, it is one of the twenty largest in the world. Look at the table below. It shows the **population** of some of the cities in the "top twenty." Can you tell by looking at the table which cities are larger than Chicago and which are smaller? How?

population, the number of people.

City	Population
Cairo	5,715,000
Chicago	6,971,200
Mexico City	11,339,774
New York	16,206,841
Peking	7,570,000

The bar graph at right shows the same thing as the table above. The difference is that the population of each city is shown by a colored bar. The numbers along the left-hand side of the graph stand for population in millions. Along the bottom are the names of the cities.

Is it easier to tell which cities are larger and smaller than Chicago by looking at the table or the graph? Why? Which gives more exact information on how many people live in each city?

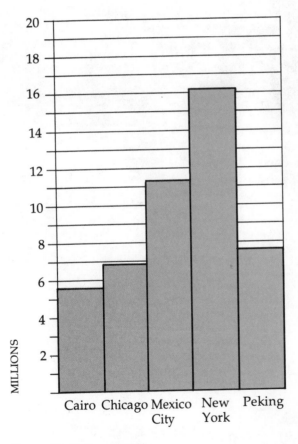

(Source: *World Almanac* 1978)

103

Lesson 2   Weather and Climate

Understanding
Sun
and rain
and wind
and storms
and thunder go together.

There has to be a little bit
of each to make the weather.

Myra Cohn Livingston

Just as the location of your community can affect your choices, so can its **weather** and **climate.** Suppose, for example, that you plan to go on a picnic Saturday. But, suppose when Saturday comes, it brings "thunder" and "storms." You decide to cancel your picnic because of bad weather. Weather has influenced your choices.

When we talk about weather we mean the day-to-day changes in the hotness, coldness, dryness, and wetness of a place. Climate means the kind of weather a place has over many months or even years.

Here is an example that will show you the difference between weather and climate. Sometimes the *weather* is very hot in Chicago. The summer Diana, Vito, Gina, and Sammy were asked to describe Chicago, temperatures rose into the high 90s on many days. (Perfect swimming weather!) But, even though the *weather* sometimes is very hot in Chicago, still we don't say that Chicago has a hot *climate.* Let's see why not.

**Chicago, Illinois
Average Monthly Temperatures**

FAHRENHEIT (Degrees)

CELSIUS (Degrees)

J F M A M J J A S O N D

Look at the graph on page 106. It shows the temperatures in Chicago over a twelve-month period. Temperatures are shown in Fahrenheit degrees on the left-hand side of the graph and in Celsius degrees on the right-hand side. The letters along the bottom stand for the months of the year.

Study the graph carefully. Do you think Gina, Vito, Diana, and Sammy would choose to go swimming in Chicago in January or February? Why or why not? When might the children go swimming?

You can see from the graph that Chicago gets very cold during the months of January and February. July and August are very hot. Chicago has a hot-cold climate.

Some places are hot year round. They have a hot climate. Some are cold for most of the year. We say they have a cold climate.

The graphs at right show the monthly temperatures of two other American cities, Fairbanks, Alaska, and Miami, Florida. Which one has a cold climate? Which has a hot climate? How are their climates different from Chicago's climate?

Fairbanks, Alaska
Average Monthly Temperatures

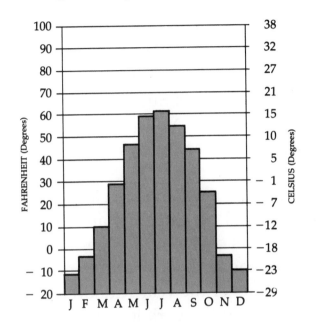

Miami, Florida
Average Monthly Temperatures

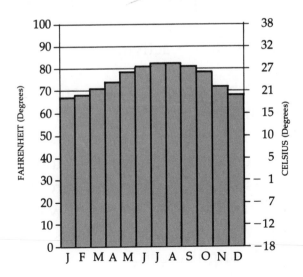

107

Seasons

When people talk about climate, they often divide the year into parts. The parts of the year are called **seasons.** In the United States, the spring season occurs during the months of March, April, and May. The summer season is June, July, and August. Fall is September, October, and November. And winter is December, January, and February.

Catoctin Mountain is a beautiful park in Maryland. The pictures on the next pages show how the park looks at different seasons of the year. Children who visit the park look forward to the changing seasons because it means they can do different things there. Read on to find out how the changing seasons affect the children's activities.

In the spring the days are warm. The children can walk in the hills and smell the wild flowers. They can listen to the birds sing. They can run through Round Meadow. They can watch the snow melt and the grass grow bright green.

108

In the summer, the days are hot. The children can fish in Owens Creek. They can pick peaches from Pleasant Valley Orchard. They can play in the water below Cunningham Falls. They can climb Wolf Rock. They can camp in the woods and sleep under the stars.

In the fall, some of the days are warm and some are chilly. The children can help pick, can, and dry fruits and vegetables. They can make apple butter. They can watch the green leaves on the trees change to red, brown, or yellow. They can run and jump in the leaves. They can take long hayrides.

In the winter, the days are chilly or cold. The children can slide or skate on the ice on Big Hunting Creek. Sometimes, they can go sledding or skiing in the hills. They can track animals in the snow. Because of the cold, the children spend less time outside. They often sit by the fire in the lodge and read or play games.

Think About It
1. How are weather and climate alike? How are they different?
2. How do weather and climate affect people's choices?
3. Name the four seasons and tell when they are in the United States.
4. How do the changing seasons affect people's choices?

Lesson 3
Natural Resources

Lake Michigan and Catoctin Mountain Park are important to the children who live near them. They help the children meet some of their needs for fresh air and **recreation.** They are important recreational resources. A **resource** supplies people with something they want or need.

Lake Michigan and Catoctin Mountain supply other wants and needs as well. Catoctin's forests are important resources. So are its fruit trees and streams filled with fish. Lake Michigan supplies the water needs of the people who live near it—and some of their food needs as well. Ships use Lake Michigan to bring goods from all over the world to the communities along Lake Michigan's shores.

recreation, fun or play.

Catoctin Mountain Park is just one of our country's thousands of state and national parks. These parklands were set aside to preserve wildlife, natural beauty, and recreational and historical areas. Opposite, an elk in Yellowstone National Park, Wyoming.

For these reasons and more, Catoctin and Lake Michigan are considered important **natural resources.** Natural resources are things found in nature that people can use.

Natural resources like water, land, forests, and wildlife are especially important. They supply people with things they need to live. Because they are so important, these resources must be used wisely. They can be used up or destroyed. When that happens, it can seriously limit people's choices. The following story will show you how.

The "Supermarket of the Plains Indians"

For over 200 years, the Cheyenne, Sioux, Pawnee, and other Indian people lived as hunters on the **Great Plains** of North America. They were buffalo hunters, and the buffalo determined their whole way of life. Each summer, the people followed the buffalo herds as they moved north over the plains. In the winter they followed the herds south again.

Great Plains, the grasslands of central and western North America.

114

ROCKY MOUNTAINS

MISSISSIPPI RIVER

Great Plains

The buffalo supplied most of the needs of the Plains Indians. Buffalo meat was their main food. Buffalo **hides,** or skins, were used for clothing, blankets, saddle cloths, and houses. Buffalo bones were made into knives, hoes, bows, and spear points. One writer called the buffalo "the supermarket of the Plains Indians."

In time, however, other people came to the land of the Plains Indians. Some of these new settlers were farmers. They fenced in the land. This meant the buffalo couldn't roam as freely as before. Other settlers were cattle ranchers and sheepherders. Their animals used the buffalo grazing lands.

Then, large numbers of white people began to hunt buffalo for sport. Sometimes, they shot the buffalo from moving trains and didn't even bother to pick up the animals they killed. The buffalo numbered almost 15 million in the 1860s. By 1875, there were less than one thousand left. With the buffalo gone, the Plains Indians had no choice. They had to give up the way of life they had followed for over two hundred years.

Think About It
1. What is a resource?
2. What are natural resources?
3. Why are things like water, land, and fish important natural resources?
4. Why were the buffalo important to the Plains Indians?
5. Why did the Indians have to give up their way of life?

A Lake Community

Larger fish

Many kinds of plants and animals live in a freshwater lake or pond. They depend on each other for food. Here's how it happens.

Sunshine helps green water plants like algae to grow. Things called carbon dioxide, nitrates, and phosphates also must be in the water for algae to grow.

Very tiny water animals, called plankton, eat the algae. Small fish, insects, and other small

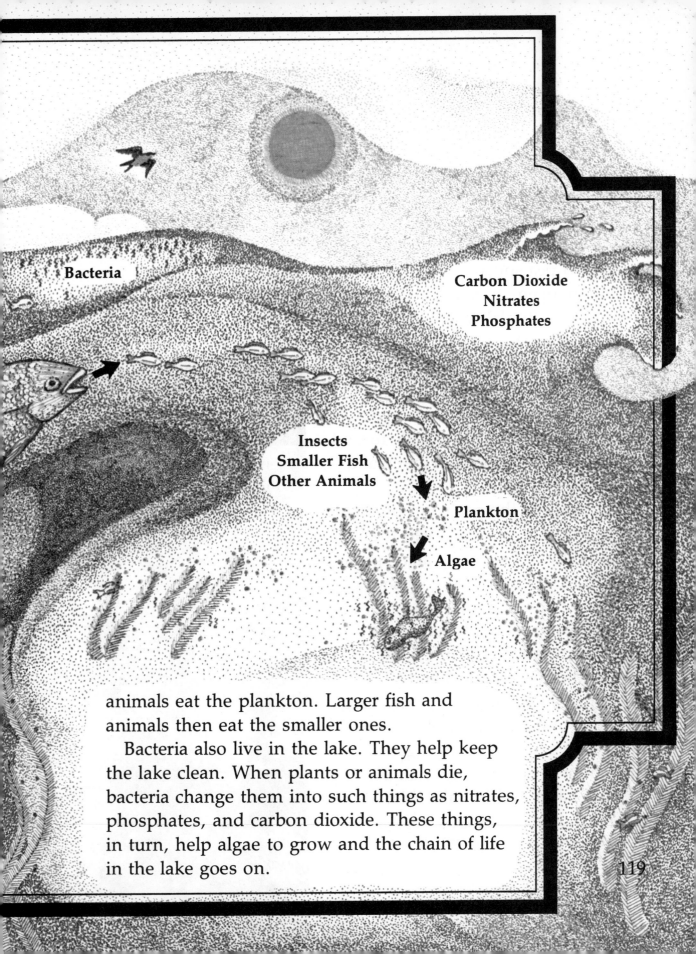

Bacteria

Carbon Dioxide
Nitrates
Phosphates

Insects
Smaller Fish
Other Animals

Plankton

Algae

animals eat the plankton. Larger fish and
animals then eat the smaller ones.

Bacteria also live in the lake. They help keep
the lake clean. When plants or animals die,
bacteria change them into such things as nitrates,
phosphates, and carbon dioxide. These things,
in turn, help algae to grow and the chain of life
in the lake goes on.

Lesson 4
The Pea Soup Problem

Imagine it is a hot summer day. You decide to go to your favorite beach for a swim. Instead of finding the clear water you usually see, however, you find the water has mysteriously turned to pea soup.

Only happens in make-believe stories, you think? Well, you would have seen just that if you tried to go swimming in parts of Lake Erie, another one of the **Great Lakes**, on a hot summer day a few years ago. Of course, the water hadn't *really* turned to pea soup. It just looked green and thick like pea soup.

What caused the pea soup problem? Huge amounts of algae filled the water. Why did so much algae grow? Look back at the drawing of the lake community on pages 118 and 119. It will help you see what happened.

You remember that things like carbon dioxide, nitrates, and phosphates help algae to grow. Large amounts of these things plus warm, sunny days can cause the algae to grow a lot faster than normal. This is what happened in Lake Erie.

Great Lakes, chain of five lakes, Superior, Michigan, Huron, Erie, Ontario, in central North America.

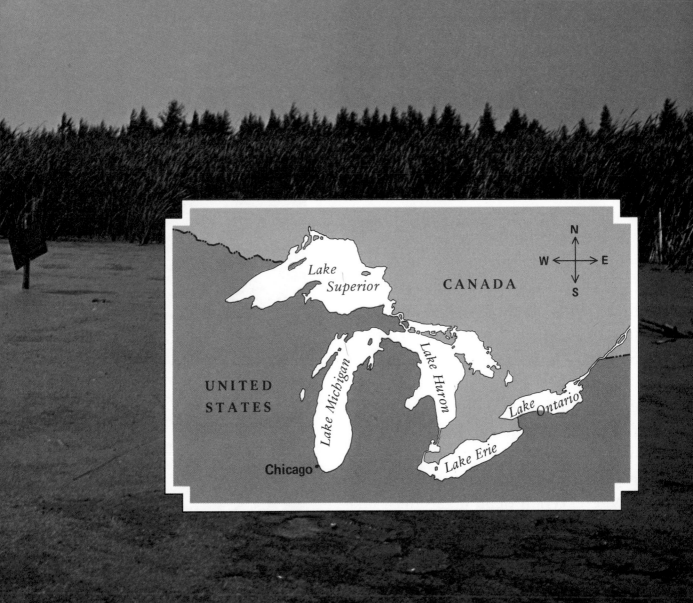

Lake Superior

CANADA

N
W ← → E
S

UNITED
STATES

Lake Michigan

Lake Huron

Lake Ontario

Lake Erie

Chicago

Not only do algae grow quickly, they die almost as fast. This causes problems that affect other parts of the chain of life in the lake community.

Look back again at pages 118 and 119. Notice that bacteria change dead plants and animals into carbon dioxide, nitrates, and phosphates. To do this, bacteria use oxygen in the lake's water. When there is a lot of dead algae in the water, the bacteria have a big job to do. They need a lot more oxygen than usual. When too much of the water's oxygen is used up, fish and other water life are in trouble. Here's why.

All living things need oxygen to stay alive. It's the oxygen in the air that allows you to breathe. (Just try to do without the air's oxygen for a few minutes by holding your breath. See how important oxygen is!)

Water has oxygen in it too—not enough for people but enough for fish and other water life. They breathe in the oxygen in the water much like you breathe in the air's oxygen. When dead algae fill a lake or pond and the bacteria must use a lot of the water's oxygen, there isn't enough for fish and other water life to use. They must leave the area or die.

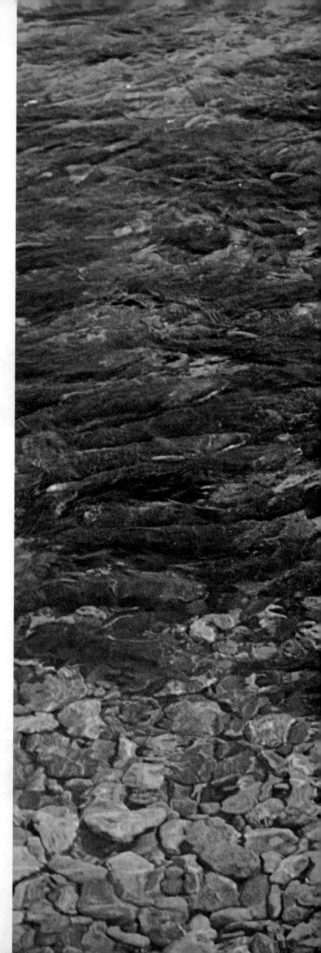

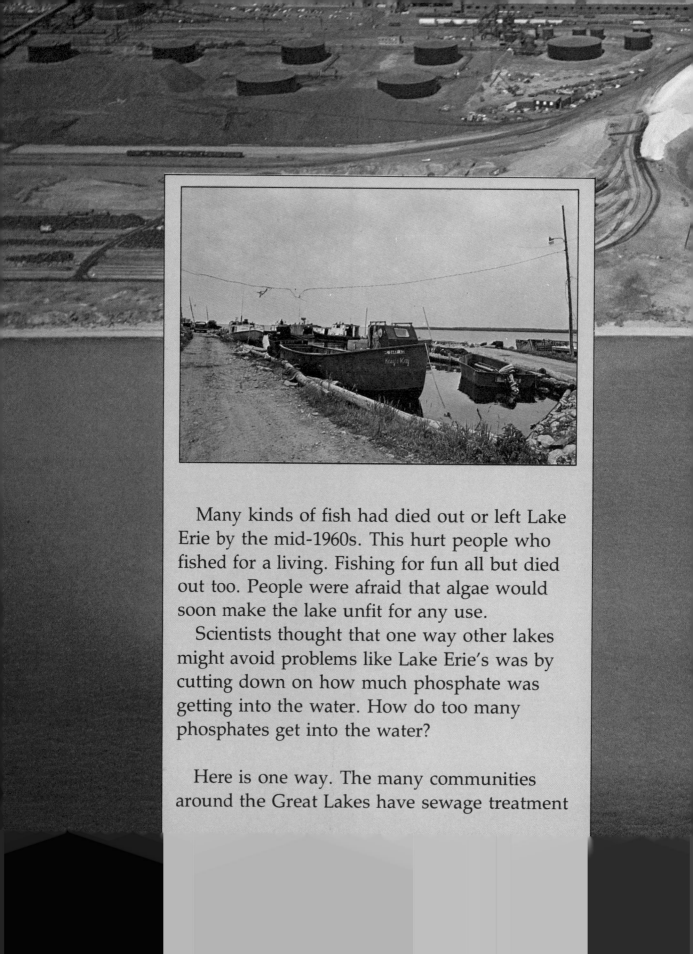

Many kinds of fish had died out or left Lake Erie by the mid-1960s. This hurt people who fished for a living. Fishing for fun all but died out too. People were afraid that algae would soon make the lake unfit for any use.

Scientists thought that one way other lakes might avoid problems like Lake Erie's was by cutting down on how much phosphate was getting into the water. How do too many phosphates get into the water?

Here is one way. The many communities around the Great Lakes have sewage treatment

plants to treat the **sewage** they produce. If these communities put raw, or untreated sewage into the lakes, the water would not be clean enough for people to use in any way. So, for many years, communities treated the sewage and turned it into phosphates. This has kept the lakes clean enough for people to drink and to use for other things. Without most people knowing it, though, a big phosphate build-up was developing in the lakes. This build-up contributed to the algae problem.

sewage, the waste matter that passes through sewers.

Sewage treatment plant in Chicago, Illinois.

You will find another big source of phosphates right in your own home. It's plain old laundry detergent. Until not too long ago, most laundry detergents had a lot of phosphates. When people use detergents, these phosphates enter the sewage system and finally are dumped into the lake.

Soon after the problems in Lake Erie became known, people in the communities around Lake Michigan noticed some of the signs of oxygen starvation in their lake. Many of the best lake fish were no longer around. Tests showed that there were a lot of phosphates in the water.

Some communities began planning the big, costly job of building new sewage treatment plants. But other communities decided that they would do something right away to cut down on the amount of phosphates going into the lake.

Chicago was the first community to act. In 1971, Chicago passed a law stopping the sale of products that had phosphates in them. Later, the states of Michigan and Indiana passed similar laws.

This means that Gina, Vito, Diana, and Sammy will not find a detergent like POW below in the neighborhood store. POW contains phosphates. They will find detergents like BAM. BAM was made without phosphates.

INGREDIENTS:
BAM contains washing soda to soften water, and linear alkylate sulfonate to provide suds and lift dirt from clothes. Sodium silicate to protect washer parts. Inorganic salts as a processing aid. Small quantities of moisture, soil suspending agents, anticaking agents, fabric whiteners, and perfume.

INGREDIENTS:
POW contains ingredients to lift dirt from clothes (anionic surfactants) and soften water (complex sodium phosphates). Sodium silicate to protect washer parts. Sodium sulfate as a processing aid, plus small quantities of moisture, soil suspending agents, anticaking agents, fabric whiteners and perfume.

PHOSPHORUS CONTENT:
This POW formula averages 6.1% phosphorus, in the form of phosphates, which is equivalent to 5.8 grams per 1¼ cup use level.

Look at the laundry detergent you have at home or look at the detergent in a local store. Which kind is sold in your community?

128

By 1977, because of this **ban** on phosphates, phosphorous levels in Lake Michigan were way down. Lake Michigan didn't have any outbreaks of algae growth like Lake Erie. And, even though Lake Michigan still faces many other problems, lake trout and other fine fish are finding the lake a safe place to live again.

Think About It

1. Why were people concerned about the growth of algae in the Great Lakes?
2. What causes algae overgrowths?
3. What are some causes of a phosphate build-up in lakes?
4. What did the people of Chicago do to cut down on the amount of phosphates getting into the lake?
5. How does the Chicago law affect the choices of people who live there?
6. How do you think the Chicago law would affect the companies that make detergents?

ban, forbid or prohibit.

What Do You Know?

Words to Know

Match the words on the left with the correct meanings on the right. Write your answers on another sheet of paper.

1. location   **a.** forbid or prohibit
2. climate   **b.** place or position of something
3. resource   **c.** the kind of weather a place has over many months or years
4. ban   **d.** supplies people with something they want or need
5. weather   **e.** parts of the year
6. boundary   **f.** day-to-day changes in the hotness, coldness, wetness, and dryness of a place
7. seasons   **g.** shows the end or limits of something

Ideas to Know

1. Different _____ have different climates.
2. For many years, the _____ supplied most of the needs of the Cheyenne, Sioux, Pawnee, and other Plains Indians.
3. The location of your _____ can influence your choices.
4. Lake Erie and Lake Michigan are two of the _____.
5. Water, forests, and wildlife are very important _____, because they supply people with things they need to stay alive.
6. The _____ are the grasslands of central and western North America.
7. A change in one part of the chain of life in a lake or pond can cause a _____ in the other parts as well.

Using What You Know

Study the following temperature graphs for two cities in the United States. Write the answers to the questions below on another sheet of paper.

**Duluth, Minnesota
Average Monthly Temperatures**

**Dallas, Texas
Average Monthly Temperatures**

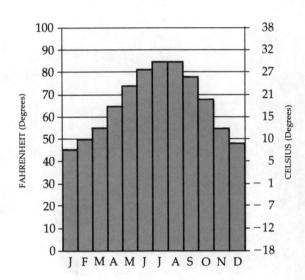

1. Which city has a cool climate?
2. Which city has a warm climate?
3. How can you tell?
4. How do you think the climate would affect the choices of people living in Dallas and Duluth?
5. Where in the United States do you think these cities are located? Why?

131

Unit 5 Communities, Past and Present

Lesson 1 People Depend on Each Other

The disappearance of the buffalo. Algae in Lake Erie. Both were caused by people upsetting the balance of nature. People did not set out to kill all the buffalo or to fill Lake Erie with algae. But, by interfering with one part of the chain of life, they upset all the other parts as well. This is because all the parts of the chain depend on each other.

social group, people who share common goals and problems.

The same is true of people's **social groups.** A change in one part of their way of living will affect all the other parts as well. You can see how this works in the social group of your own family.

Suppose, for example, that your mother has just taken a job outside the home. Up until now, she has been doing most of the work around the house for your family. Her return to work might mean that your older brother will have to come home right after school to watch the younger children in your family. Maybe you will have to spend your Saturday mornings helping clean the house. Your father might have to cook more dinners than he did before.

A change in your mother's life has affected the lives of all the other members of the family as well. This is because people in families are **interdependent**.

interdependent, depending on one another.

People in families are interdependent. So are people in larger social groups. The following story will show how.

134

Where Will They Walk?

All the children in this neighborhood in Anytown, U.S.A., had to walk in the street to get to school and back. There weren't any sidewalks where they lived. This caused lots of problems. The children had to be on the lookout all the time for cars and trucks as they walked. On rainy days, the sides of the streets would fill with water. And, since it was dangerous to walk in the center of the street, the children had no choice but to walk in the water. (Some of them didn't really mind this too much.) But their parents did—especially if the weather was cold or if their children had the sniffles.

So the people in the neighborhood got together and decided to build some sidewalks for the children.

136

The people in the first house built their part of the sidewalk out of cement they had left over from making their patio. The people in the second house made theirs out of some concrete blocks they had from building their house. The retired woman in the third house decided she could not afford to build a sidewalk. (She had just gotten a big roof repair bill.) So she told the children they could walk on her grass instead. The people in the last house had a nice hedge along the street. They didn't want to tear it out. So they decided not to build their part of the sidewalk at all.

The people in the neighborhood weren't happy with the results of their sidewalk building project. The children still had to walk in the street part of the way to school. And the new sidewalk certainly didn't add anything to the looks of the neighborhood!

Then one neighbor, Mr. Sanders, had a suggestion. "Why don't we hire someone to build the sidewalks? We can share the cost of building them. And they will look *so* nice, I'm sure everyone in the neighborhood will want them."

Everyone thought that was a fine idea. So the neighbors told Mr. Sanders to find out what it would cost to have a cement company lay sidewalks in the neighborhood. Mr. Sanders found out. It cost too much!

Then Mrs. Russo had an idea. She said, "Children walking in the street is a safety problem not only for the people in our neighborhood, but for anyone driving through our neighborhood. So it's a *community* safety problem. The whole community should help us build our sidewalks. Let's suggest that at the next town meeting."

At the town meeting, Mrs. Russo told the story of the sidewalks. After she finished, a man from another neighborhood stood up and said, "We have the same problem in our neighborhood. If town money is used to build sidewalks in your neighborhood, it should be used to build some in ours too!"

Then one of the town officials said, "Now slow down a minute everyone! Sidewalks can't be built with town money *anywhere*.

"First, the townspeople will have to vote on whether we should spend town money on sidewalks. Second, since we don't have enough money to pay for sidewalks in *both* neighborhoods, the townspeople will have to choose the neighborhood where we will build the sidewalks."

"Or," added another town official, "we can ask the townspeople if they want to have their **taxes** raised a little so we can help pay for new sidewalks in *both* neighborhoods."

taxes, money paid by people for new roads, police protection, and so on.

There is a happy ending to this sidewalk story. The townspeople voted "yes" to having the town help pay for the sidewalks. And they voted "yes" to higher taxes. So both neighborhoods got sidewalks.

Now the children in the neighborhood have drier feet and fewer cases of the sniffles. Parents don't have to worry about children walking in the street. And drivers don't have to worry about hitting children. The neighborhood looks nice again. And everybody is happy—except, perhaps, the people in the fourth house. They miss their hedge. But they're working on a new one.

Think About It

1. How are people in families interdependent?
2. Tell how the people in the neighborhood with the sidewalk problem were interdependent.
3. How did a problem in one neighborhood of Anytown affect the whole community?
4. How did the new sidewalks affect people in the neighborhood social group? The people in the community social group?
5. Give an example of a change in the social group of your family, neighborhood, or community that brought other changes as well.

City Governments

The people of Anytown talked about their sidewalk problem at a town meeting. This means Anytown has what is called a *town meeting* kind of **government.** (Government means the way a town, city, state, or country is ruled.) In towns with this plan of government, the townspeople hold a meeting one or more times a year to decide important questions facing their community.

At the meeting, the townspeople discuss their problems and pass laws for the community. They also elect town officials, sometimes called a board of selectmen, to run the town until the next meeting.

These officials watch over the different city services, such as building and planning, fire and police, streets, parks, the library, and so on. They also make sure the laws passed at the town meeting are carried out.

Usually you only can find a town meeting kind of government in a small community. (Can you think why?) Most big cities have a *mayor-council* plan of city government. Under this plan of government, the people who can vote elect a city council and a mayor. The city council discusses problems facing the community and passes laws. The mayor makes sure that the laws the council passes are carried out. He runs the city through the people he appoints as the heads of the various city service departments. Here's how the mayor-council form of government works.

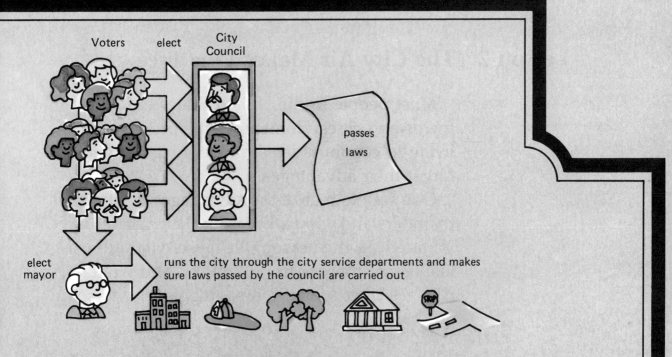

Voters — elect — City Council — passes laws

elect mayor — runs the city through the city service departments and makes sure laws passed by the council are carried out

Other cities have a *council-manager* plan of government. Under this plan, the council hires a city manager to run the city. The city manager does many of the same jobs as the mayor.

Look closely at the drawings showing the different kinds of city government. How are all the plans alike? How are they different? Which plan does your community have?

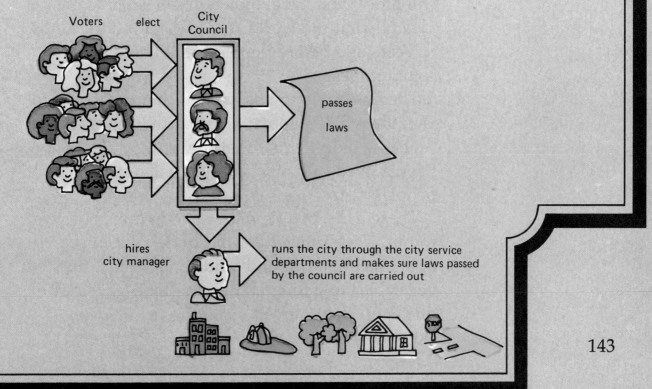

Voters — elect — City Council — passes laws

hires city manager — runs the city through the city service departments and makes sure laws passed by the council are carried out

Lesson 2 The City Air Makes One Free

Most people in the United States today live in towns and cities. Sometimes the problems of living in communities seem very big. People forget their advantages.

One way to realize the advantages of city life is to understand what life was like before cities were founded. In this lesson, we'll see what life was like before there were any cities. And what changes cities brought in people's lives and social groups.

Have you ever been in a place far, far out in the country? A place where you couldn't see any houses or cars or roads or telephones? A place where days would pass before you'd see another person besides the people you were with? A place where you were surrounded by forests and wildlife? If you have, then you can begin to get an idea of what the world was like many thousands of years ago before people started settling in communities.

There were no towns or cities then. Not one. In fact, the whole population of Earth in those times probably didn't equal that of Chicago today! People lived in family groups of about 20 to 30 people.

These early people didn't live in one spot year round. They moved around quite a bit in search of animals to hunt and wild roots, fruits, and vegetables to gather. When the food gave out in one spot, they moved on to the next.

People lived this hunting and gathering way of life for over one million years. It was only about 10,000 years ago that they began settling down in cities. Cities were the first large social groups people formed.

One reason cities grew was because people discovered how to grow their own crops and to raise animals. This meant that not all people had to wander about in search of food. Some had a sure supply right in their own backyards.

Thousands of years ago, hunting people drew this buffalo on a rock wall in the Sahara, the great desert of North Africa. Then, the Sahara probably was a green and fertile place filled with wildlife.

Egyptian people living more than 6,000 years ago knew how to grow, harvest, and process grain as this ancient painting shows.

The people who lived in the very first cities either grew their own food or traded with nearby farmers for it. What did cities have to trade with farmers? Sometimes cities had control of an important resource that people needed or wanted, like the only water or salt for miles around. (People need salt in their diet and to season and preserve their food.)

Many cities grew up where two roads crossed or a road and river met. They were natural gathering spots for people in the area around them. Farmers came to these centers to try to trade their farm goods for other things they needed. And people who had special skills gathered there to trade their **products**—woven baskets, wood bowls, pottery, knives, spears, axes, farm tools—for farm goods.

product, something people make or grow.

The growth of cities brought big changes in the world. After cities were founded, there was a big increase in the world's population. Life in cities was safer. It was easier on people, especially the old and weak, than the wandering life of a hunter. People began to live longer and not so many babies died at birth.

Also cities opened up a whole new world of choices to people. A saying grew up about the cities of later times. It was, "The city air makes one free." In one way, it can apply to the first cities too. The growth of cities meant that people were free to choose from a wide variety of roles and jobs. Cities meant that not every person born into this world had to be a hunter or farmer.

Think About It

1. Why did cities grow?
2. How did the growth of cities change people's way of living?
3. How were people in cities interdependent?

Lesson 3 Rooftop Sidewalks, Houses Without Doors

What was life like in the first cities? **Archaeologists**, the people who study the things left behind by people who lived long ago, have found some answers.

They have found the remains of Catal Hüyük (shä täl′ hü′yük′), one of the world's oldest cities, in the dry and rugged land of Central Turkey. Nine thousand years ago, from 3,000 to 6,000 people lived in Catal Hüyük. Then, this part of Turkey was covered with green forests filled with wildlife. The people of Catal Hüyük used wood from these forests to build their houses.

At first, the houses of Catal Hüyük puzzled archaeologists. The houses, made of mud crisscrossed with wood beams, usually were built close together around courtyards. But no windows or doors opened onto the courtyards. The only openings in these houses were holes near the roofs.

Archaeologists believe that the people of Catal Hüyük entered and left their houses by climbing ladders to these rooftop holes. These rooftop doors probably suited the needs of the people very well. They kept out floodwaters, wild animals, and enemies. And the rooftops of the closely built houses became the city's sidewalks!

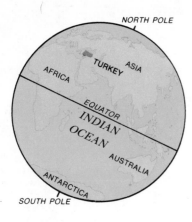

The inside of Catal Hüyük houses was very simple. They almost all had two raised wooden platforms. These served the families as tables, beds, couches, and chairs. A small oven in the wall and a food storage hole completed the furnishings of the houses.

What were the people of Catal Hüyük like? From bones found in the ruins of the city, it appears that they lived long and full lives. Men probably lived to the ripe old age of 28 (a big improvement over hunting times)! Most of the women didn't have it as good. Many of them died much younger in childbirth.

Catal Hüyük offered its people many career choices. It was an important center for trade. The women and men of Catal Hüyük used the resources of the nearby forests to make wooden bowls and woven baskets. Pottery and stone bowls were found in the ruins. So were jewelry, tools, and finely worked weapons.

Necklaces and bracelets carved from stone or from the teeth, tusks, or bones of animals were found in Catal Hüyük.

150

One of many huge bulls, painted on the walls of religious shrines in Catal Hüyük—probably to bring good luck in hunting.

Obsidian mirror, found at Catal Hüyük.

The people of Catal Hüyük still depended on wild plants and animals for much of their food. But seeds and animal bones found in the ruins show that they also had learned how to grow some of their own crops and to raise cattle.

Two other things helped Catal Hüyük grow and become rich. One of them was a nearby volcano called Hasan Dag today. Having a volcano nearby might not seem like a resource to you, but it was in **ancient** times.

ancient, belonging to times long ago.

When they erupt, volcanoes produce a shiny, black stone called obsidian (ob sid′ ē ən). Obsidian was much in demand in ancient times. For one thing, ancient people used it for mirrors. (They hadn't discovered how to make glass yet.) It also was used for jewelry and weapons.

151

The people of Catal Hüyük gave thanks for a successful harvest by placing offerings of food before these leopards in one of the city's shrines.

Catal Hüyük also served the surrounding area as a religious center. Many of the buildings found there were religious shrines. In them, the people of Catal Hüyük honored things in the world around them, things that made their life so good—the nearby volcano and the rich land they lived in.

People made their homes in Catal Hüyük for over one thousand years. Then, suddenly the city was mysteriously destroyed. Archaeologists can tell that a great fire swept through the city. There also are signs that enemies attacked the city. Perhaps they attacked Catal Hüyük killing most of the people and then set fire to the city. No one knows for sure. The answer lies buried with the people who lived there so long ago.

Living in cities brought many changes in people's way of living. It also taught them skills that, in time, enabled them to form still larger social groups. You might say that the first cities were the great-great-great-great-great-great-great-great-grandparents of the large social groups, called **nations,** that most people live in today.

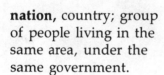

A carefully carved dagger, probably used in religious ceremonies rather than as a weapon.

nation, country; group of people living in the same area, under the same government.

Think About It
1. How was life in Catal Hüyük different from life in cities today?
2. How was it the same?
3. Why do you think people wanted to live there?
4. How do you think the people in Catal Hüyük and the people who lived in the countryside around it were interdependent?
5. Why did Catal Hüyük grow and become rich?

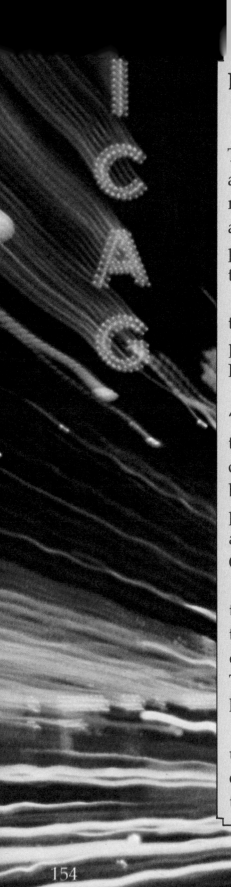

Lesson 4   Cities, Towns, Suburbs

The cities of ancient times were very simple. The homes and courtyards of Catal Hüyük were also its factories, churches, and stores. People made baskets, wooden bowls, obsidian jewelry, and weapons right in their own homes. They probably sold them in their courtyards or on those rooftop sidewalks.

Today cities are big and **complex.** This means that they are made up of many different zones, or parts. Each zone has its own special purposes. Each has its own sights and sounds.

What do you think of when you hear the word, "city"? If you're like most people, what will come to mind is a picture of that crowded area in the center of the city, made up of shiny skyscrapers, busy streets, and big department stores. You probably call it "downtown" or "the city." It's also called the "central business district," or the C.B.D.

Thousands of people pour into the C.B.D. of the nation's large cities every day. They go there to shop in the stores, to work in the skyscraper office buildings, to eat in the many restaurants. They go to see movies, plays, sports events, to hear concerts, and to visit museums.

The crush of people and traffic in the C.B.D. usually makes it a very noisy place. But it's a very exciting place too. One writer felt this way about the noisy downtown area:

City sounds are noisy sounds
Wherever you may be:
The roar of cars, the screech of tires
A downtown symphony.

(Pictures from left to right) An industrial area of Chicago; rowhouses in the Bronx, New York City; suburban housing; farmhouse in a rural area.

But there are other parts of cities besides the downtown area. In some parts, factories and warehouses line the streets. There you'll hear the noise of machines, see trucks being loaded and unloaded. Factory smells might fill the air. You are in the **industrial** part of the city.

Other parts of the city are mostly **residential.** These are where people reside, or live. Some residential areas are filled with skyscraper apartment buildings. Others are made up of smaller apartment buildings, city rowhouses, or single-family homes. In some of these neighborhoods, the houses start at the sidewalk's edge. In others, the houses have big yards and the streets are lined with trees.

There is less noise and traffic in these residential parts of the city. What you might hear are the sounds of children playing on the sidewalks in front of their buildings. The sounds of a person practicing a clarinet. A new baby crying. A father calling his children home for supper. The clatter of pots and pans in kitchens. This is the city neighborhood "symphony."

156

The **urban** area also includes the **suburbs** and small towns that border the city. Many people who live there travel into the city to work each day and return home at night. Some of these communities are new. They were built just to house the overflow of people as the city grew larger. Other communities are older. They became part of the urban area as the city grew out to them. These suburban towns have many different kinds of buildings—houses, apartments, businesses, stores, and schools. They're smaller copies of cities.

It's quieter in most suburban communities than in cities. The sounds you hear are lawnmowers buzzing, neighbors calling to each other over hedges or fences, children shouting at play.

Outside urban areas you can go for miles without seeing a town or a city. These are the **rural** areas where you see planted fields, orchards, forests. It's quiet there. Instead of traffic and lawnmowers, you might hear birds singing and wind blowing through trees. When the road does wind into a town, it's a small community like the Amish one discussed in Unit 3.

urban, having to do with a city.

suburbs, towns or areas just outside or near a city.

rural, in the country.

People who live in the suburbs and work in the city often travel to and from their jobs on "commuter" trains like this one.

Where Americans Choose to Live

Today *most* Americans live in urban areas, that is, in cities and their suburbs. The chief reason for this is that there is a wider choice of jobs in urban areas.

Many things can influence where people choose to live in the urban area. Sometimes people choose to live in the suburbs because they don't like the noise and crowding of the city. Or, they think suburbs have less crime and better schools than the city.

Some people choose the city because they think it's an exciting place to live. They like all the different kinds of people and all the things they can do there. Other people choose the city because they have to. Perhaps they can't afford the cost of suburban housing. Or, if they work in the city, they might not be able to afford the cost of a car or daily train and bus rides from the suburbs to their job.

Look at the bar graphs at right. They show the number of people in city and suburban areas in 1960 and 1970. Which gained more people between 1960 and 1970—cities or suburbs?

If you said suburbs have gained more people than cities, you were right. But some people think that a new movement of people back into the cities will occur in the 1980s.

Like so many other Americans, Inez and Charles McCord joined the move to the suburbs. But, in 1977, they moved back into the city. They chose to leave the comfortable suburb of Ford City on the southwest side of Chicago to settle in the city neighborhood where they grew up. Why?

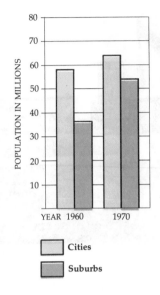

POPULATION IN MILLIONS

YEAR 1960   1970

☐ Cities
☐ Suburbs

Charles and Inez McCord on the steps of their remodeled city townhouse.

159

The McCords shown in the living room, library, and kitchen of their remodeled home.

"I guess we're getting back to our roots here," Charles McCord said looking around his new/old neighborhood.

But the city neighborhood the McCords returned to wasn't the same as the one they grew up in. The McCords' old neighborhood, like many in the city, was in bad shape. Some houses stood empty. Others, including the McCords' house, were in ruins with broken pipes, broken windows, and holes in the walls. This has happened in city neighborhoods across the country as people have moved out of cities to the suburbs. The poorer people who are left in the city often can't keep up these neighborhoods.

The McCord house was about to be torn down by the city wrecking crew when the McCords decided to spend their savings to fix it up.

"We felt this old home was too good to waste," Inez McCord said.

"Where else can you get 12-inch walls and 9½-foot ceilings for under $50,000?" Charles McCord added.

160

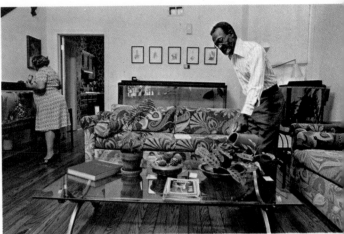

Now the McCords' brick townhouse is the showplace of the neighborhood. It has encouraged their neighbors to make their own beautification efforts.

The McCords are happy they made the choice they did. Charles McCord said, "It's a shame that more people who could really do something to improve the inner city turn their backs on it."

Think About It

1. Describe the different parts of the city.
2. How are cities and suburbs interdependent? Urban and rural areas?
3. "All suburbs are alike." Is this statement true or not true? Explain.
4. Which gained more people in recent years—cities or suburbs?
5. Name some things that might influence people's choices about where they live in the urban area.
6. "People moved to cities because it was so much better than living in the country." Tell why you agree or disagree with this statement.

When You Read Social Studies

Mapmakers use small drawings, or symbols, to stand for different things when they make their maps. A map symbol is a drawing which stands for something real on the Earth's surface. In order to read maps, you should know some map symbols.

The two symbols below stand for water. The color blue often means water. Look at the picture of the river. Then, read the symbol for river. Look at the picture of the lake. Then, read the symbol for lake.

River    Lake

Other symbols stand for things that people have built. Look at each photo. Read the symbols. What other things are made by people?

Highway, Street, or Road

Railroad

Airport

Bridge

This map shows the large city of Centerville and some places near it. Look at the map key. It will help you read the map. The key tells you what each symbol on the map stands for.

The map also has a sign to show directions. Can you find the sign that shows direction on the map? What direction does the letter N stand for?

Find Centerville. How is its size and shape shown on the map? How many main highways cross Centerville?

Find the suburb of New Town. What direction is it from Centerville? What suburb is on the main highway north of Centerville? In which direction do people go to get from Willow Grove to Springfield?

Find Deep River. How many bridges cross the river? Which suburbs are east of the river? Which ones are west of the river?

How many lakes are there on the map? Is Pine Lake north or south of Mapleton?

How many railroads cross the map? Which suburbs are on a railroad?

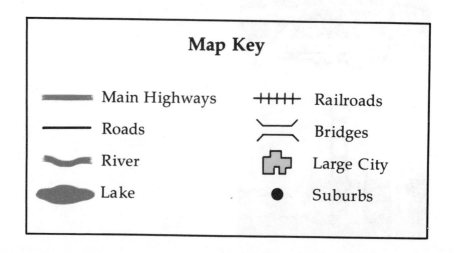

Map Key

━━━ Main Highways	++++ Railroads
—— Roads	⁓ Bridges
～ River	⬩ Large City
⬮ Lake	● Suburbs

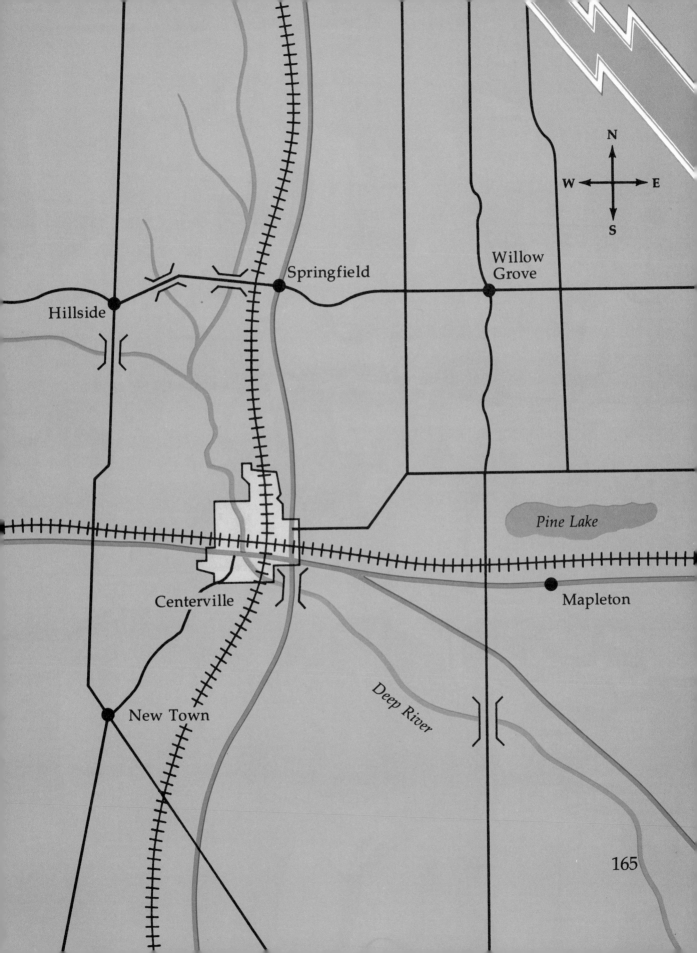

Hillside

Springfield

Willow
Grove

N
W   E
S

Pine Lake

Centerville

Mapleton

Deep River

New Town

165

Lesson 5 From Sheep to Cloth

Meet Mrs. Payne's class. They had some questions. They found some answers and they want to share them with you.

One day Mrs. Payne asked her class: "Does anyone know what clothes are made of?" Bret said, "I know. They're made of cloth."

"That's right," Mrs. Payne said. "Does anyone know where cloth comes from?" No one knew. Then Mrs. Payne showed the class a label in her coat. She said, "Labels in clothes tell you what they are made of. Clothes can be made from many different kinds of cloth. This label says that this coat is made of wool cloth. Who knows where wool comes from?"

Ricky knew that wool comes from sheep. Mrs. Payne showed the class a picture of a farmer cutting the wool off a sheep. Wool, just as it comes off the sheep's back, is called **raw wool.**

167

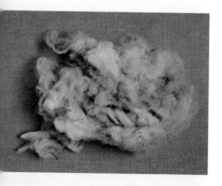

Mrs. Payne brought in some raw wool from a woolen mill in town. When the children looked at it under a magnifying glass, they found that it was made up of tiny, hairlike strands called **fibers.**

Becky asked how the dirty, smelly raw wool could ever be turned into a beautiful coat. "Let's find out how wool cloth is made by making some right here in the classroom," Mrs. Payne said.

So the class project began. The class learned that first the dirty raw wool has to be washed. Then it is **carded.**

This means the fibers are untangled and made to lie down flat in one direction. Carded wool is then made into long, loose, fluffy ropes.

The class could see that there were going to be many steps to turning raw wool into cloth. The children decided to make a bulletin board to keep track of all the steps.

(Pictures from top to bottom) Raw or unwashed wool; washed wool; carded wool. (At right) Carded wool made into long, fluffy ropes.

Mrs. Payne showed the children how they could card wool themselves and then spin it into **yarn.**

First, the children learned how to card wool by hand. They pulled raw wool through the carding tool until it lay straight and flat.

Next, Mrs. Payne showed the children how to make their own spindles for spinning the carded wool into yarn. For their spindles, the class used potatoes and pieces of wood 8 inches (20 centimeters) long. They cut notches in the tops of their pieces of wood and then pushed them through the potatoes.

Next, the children twisted some of the carded wool in their fingers and tied it onto the notches of their spindles. Then, they brought the wool down under the potatoes, wrapped it around their spindles, then brought it back to the tops of their spindles where they looped it around the notches and tied it.

Then the children were ready to start their spinning. Holding their spindles by the ropes of carded wool, the children spun them around. As the spindles turned, the weight of the potatoes stretched the wool into thinner and thinner strands until it became yarn. As their strands of yarn lengthened, the children unfastened their loops, wrapped the spun yarn around the spindles above the potatoes, and continued spinning.

At right is some of the yarn the children spun. The children dyed some of their yarn after it was spun. The class learned that many things found around the home—like tea and dried onion skins—can be used to dye yarn.

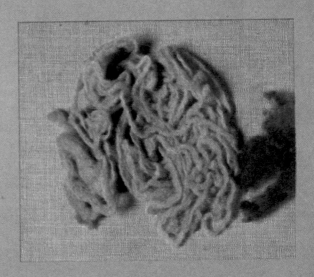

The next step in turning wool into cloth is **weaving.** Weaving means twisting and tying the threads of yarn together so they become one whole piece of material. To weave you must have a **loom,** or frame to tie the yarn to.

The children made their looms of cardboard cut into pieces about 4 inches by 5 inches (10 centimeters by 12.5). They placed toothpicks in the narrow end of the cardboard.

Next, they tied one end of yarn to a toothpick and pulled the yarn down around the bottom of the cardboard, up the opposite side, and around the next toothpick. Then they took the yarn down the same side of the cardboard, up the first side, and around the next toothpick. They continued in the same way until they reached the last toothpick. Then they tied the yarn and cut it.

For the next step in the weaving process, Mrs. Payne brought in some ice cream sticks. In each one, she had drilled a hole about ⅛th of an inch wide. The class used these as **shuttles.** The children threaded their shuttles with a 2 to 3 foot length of yarn. They wove this thread over and under the lengthwise threads on their looms.

Some children used two or more colors of yarn to make their patterns.

When they were finished, they removed their yarn from their looms and turned it inside out so their knots wouldn't show.

Some children braided drawstrings, threaded them through the loops on their woven cloth, and knotted the ends. They had little coin purses or treasure bags to use themselves or to give as gifts.

175

From Woolen Mill to You

Mrs. Payne's class wanted to find out how wool from sheep is turned into cloth. Every child got a chance to turn a piece of raw wool into woven cloth.

Making woolen cloth in a mill is different in some ways from the way the children made theirs. First, woolen mills have big machines that do the carding, spinning, and weaving much faster than it can be done by hand. Second, different workers in a woolen mill work on different parts of the clothmaking job. One group of people works on the carding machines; another on the machines that spin the wool into yarn, and so on. This way the mill can produce goods much faster than if one person took one piece of wool through all the steps in clothmaking.

The people who work at the various jobs in a woolen mill are interdependent. And the mill itself is part of another interdependent **system.**

system, set of things or parts that make up a whole.

(Pictures from top to bottom) A carding machine at a South Carolina mill; spinning machines; weaving looms.

Mr. Walsh's class traced the system that the woolen mill in their town is part of on a map. Here's how it works. Some raw wool comes to the mill from such states as Arizona, Colorado, Idaho, and Utah. The mill also gets some wool from such places as Australia and New Zealand. After the raw wool is turned into cloth, it goes to clothing manufacturers in New York, Los Angeles, and Chicago. From the clothing manufacturers it goes to the department stores and then to you.

Think About It
1. List the steps in the woolmaking process.
2. How can you tell what your clothes are made of?
3. How is clothmaking different in a mill?
4. Why would a mill want a way of producing wool very quickly?
5. How are workers in a woolen mill interdependent? How is the mill part of a larger interdependent system?

Buyers Beware

The next time you're getting ready for school take a look in the collar of your shirt or sweater. Do you see a label there that tells you what the shirt or sweater is made of? You should. That's the law!

According to the Fair Packaging and Labeling Act, there must be a label on all the food and clothing we buy. The label must:

1. Be printed so people can read it.
2. Be placed where people can find it easily.
3. Tell what is in the product.

The law also says that labels must provide honest information about the product. For example, such things as the true size and weight of the product must be clearly marked on the package. Because of this law, you won't be faced with the following situation which buyers encountered in the past.

You go to the store to buy a package of hot dogs. One package you pick up says "jumbo pound." Another just says "pound." They both cost the same. Which would you buy?

Most people probably would buy the "jumbo pound" because it sounds as if you get more. But actually both packages only contain one pound. The makers of the "jumbo pound" hot dogs are trying to make you think you get more than a pound. This kind of dishonest labeling now is forbidden by law.

The law also says that the labels of some products must contain a list of *ingredients* (what the product is made of) by *quantity* (amount). Look at the list of ingredients below from a leading breakfast cereal. The cereal is called a "wheat" cereal. So you would expect wheat to be the first ingredient on the list, right? Wrong. What is the first ingredient on the list? It's sugar. That means that this cereal has more sugar than wheat in it. Probably it should call itself a sugar cereal!

Check the ingredient lists on the cereal boxes in your grocery store. How many should call themselves "sugar" cereals?

INGREDIENTS: SUGAR, WHEAT, CORN SYRUP, PARTIALLY HYDROGENATED SOYBEAN OIL, HONEY, SALT, CARAMEL COLORING, SODIUM ACETATE, SODIUM ASCORBATE (C), VITAMIN A PALMITATE, NIACINAMIDE, REDUCED IRON, LECITHIN, PYRIDOXINE HYDROCHLORIDE (B_6), RIBOFLAVIN (B_2), THIAMIN HYDROCHLORIDE (B_1), FOLIC ACID AND VITAMIN D_2.

NUTRITION INFORMATION PER SERVING

Serving Size: 1 ounce (about 1 cup)
Servings per Container: 12

	1 oz. pep POPS	pep POPS plus ½ cup vit. D Milk
Calories	110	190
Protein, grams	3	7
Carbohydrate, grams	23	29
Fat, grams	1	5

Percentage of U.S. Recommended Daily Allowances (U.S. RDA)

Protein	4	10
Vitamin A	25	30
Vitamin C	25	25
Thiamin	25	30
Riboflavin	25	35
Niacin	25	25

179

What Do You Know?

Words to Know

Match the words on the left with the correct meanings on the right. Write your answers on another sheet of paper.

1. social group
2. product
3. nation
4. taxes
5. interdependent

a. depending on one another
b. country; group of people living in the same area under the same government
c. people who have common goals or problems
d. something people make or grow
e. money paid by people to run the government

Ideas to Know

Number a paper from 1 to 4. Write the letter of the correct answer on your paper.

1. You live with twenty-five relatives. You don't live in one spot year round. Instead you move about in search of food. Where do you live? **(a)** In one of the first cities **(b)** In a hunting band in the days before cities were founded **(c)** In a city today

2. Factories and warehouses line the streets. Where are you? **(a)** In the central business district of a big city **(b)** In an industrial area of a city **(c)** In a suburban area

3. You travel downtown to work each day on the train. It's a forty-five minute trip each way. But you don't mind. You like coming home to your quiet neighborhood. Where do you live? **(a)** In an industrial area of the city **(b)** In the C.B.D. **(c)** In the suburbs

4. You're excited about going hunting with the grown-ups. You strap on your new knife. You grab some cold wheat cakes from the food storage hole to eat on the way. You climb the ladder to the door of your house. Outside you run to where the other hunters stand waiting. Where are you? **(a)** In a hunting band in the times before cities were founded **(b)** In the city of Catal Hüyük **(c)** In Chicago today

Using What You Know

Match the pictures on the left with the correct symbols on the right. Write your answers on another sheet of paper.

1.

a.

2.

b.

3.

c.

181

Unit 6 Different Communities, Different Choices

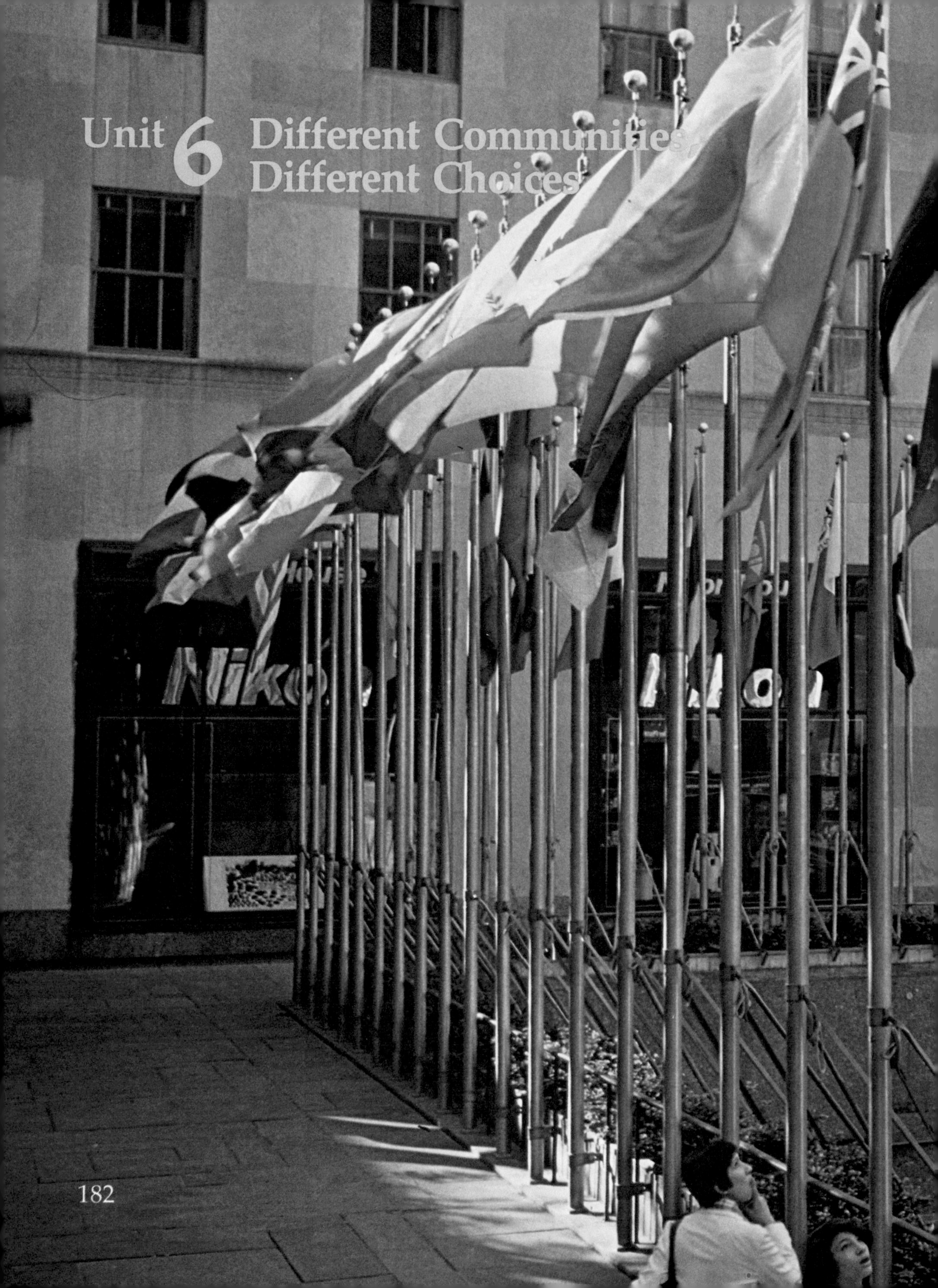

183

Lesson 1 Starting from Scratch

Day 1 The storm lasted three days and three nights. I have never seen waves so huge. Our ship was smashed to bits. We held onto our life boats for what seemed like forever. Then finally we spotted land. I can't describe how it felt to stand on solid ground. Many of us had wondered if we would ever know that feeling again. I guess this place—wherever it is—is home for the time being.

Day 2 The captain sent out a group to explore. We are on a small island. No signs of other people. There is little food—a few coconut palms, some banana trees. We've seen some birds and a few monkeys, no other animals. It rained this afternoon just as it did yesterday.

Day 5 All of us have been hunting for food in the mornings. In the afternoons, we've been trying to gather things to make houses. We badly need protection from this never ending rain. Yesterday and today we returned to camp to find much of our food gone. Captain Fraser thinks maybe the monkeys are stealing it.

Day 10 Food still disappearing. So we all met to decide what to do. Captain Fraser had a plan all worked out. He divided us into four groups. Each group was given a certain job to do. One is to do the food gathering, another the house building.

One group is to stay at camp to keep watch over the food. A fourth is to take care of building a fire that will be a signal to passing ships.

Day 15 The signal people let the fire go out. They went swimming instead. It was hard to start the fire again. The fire wood was wet from the afternoon rain.

Day 20 No problems these last few days. Maybe the captain's plan will work.

I've walked all over the island now. This is how it looks.

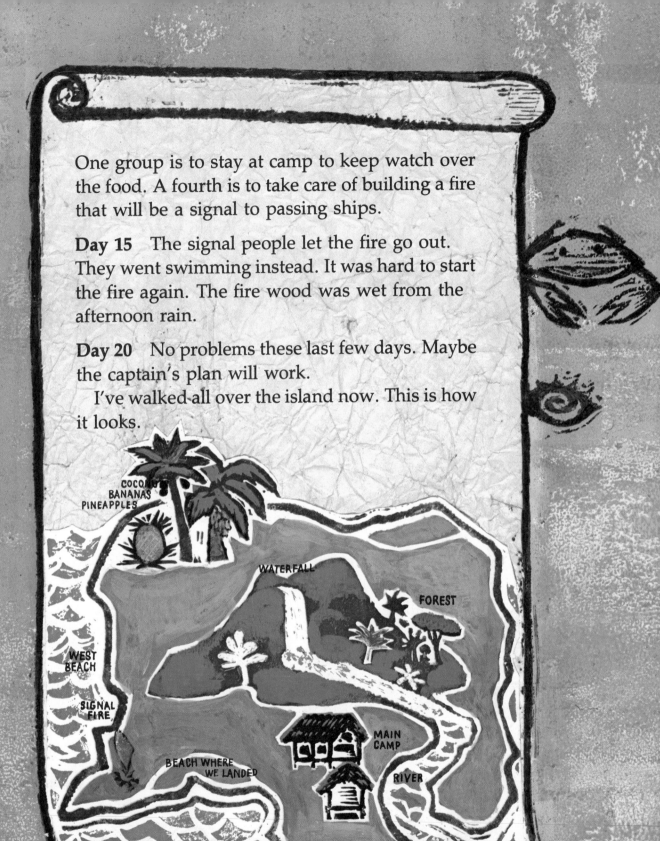

Day 25   Trouble today. The group that's supposed to gather food took time out to explore some caves. They didn't bring back enough food. Many of us went hungry. The captain said that maybe there should be some kind of punishment for those who don't do their jobs. Some people agreed. Others got angry. "We're tired of following your rules," they said. "You never asked *us* what we thought of your rules. Who asked you to be leader anyway? We're not on the ship anymore, you know."

Then one person, Russell Armstrong, said, "Well, we should choose a leader, and we should vote on what rules to follow. I think we food gatherers work harder than anybody else. We should have two votes apiece. Others should only have one."

"That's not fair!" the others cried. "Who says food gatherers work harder than the rest of us? We all have a right to vote equally in whatever we do."

Day 26   Nobody could agree last night. Today all work has stopped. What are we going to do?

Groups often need rules. Rules can help people get along together. Rules help people get things done more quickly and simply. They can keep people from redoing the same things.

There are all kinds of rules. One set of rules might be fair to everybody. Another might be fair to only a few. Think about the rule Russell Armstrong suggested. Was it fair to everybody? Are there any rules that would be fair to all?

A Plan of Government

More than 300 years ago, people from other countries started **colonies** in our land. Colonies are groups of communities in one country that are ruled by another country. Spain, France, and Holland all had colonies in North America. England gained control of the Thirteen Colonies along the eastern coast of North America. These colonies came to have the most settlers in them.

For about 100 years, France, England, and Spain had large colonies in North America. But by 1763, the English and the Spanish gained control of most of the land.

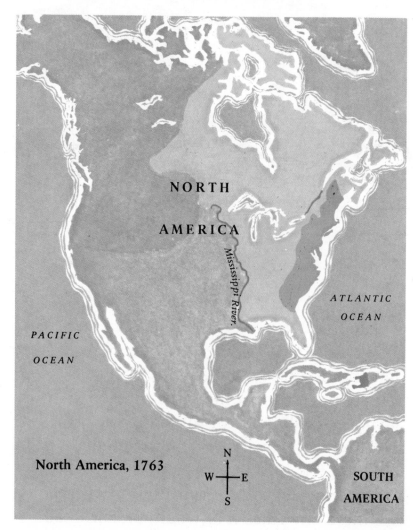

KEY

Thirteen Colonies

English

French

Spanish

Unclaimed by Europeans

NORTH

AMERICA

Mississippi River

PACIFIC OCEAN

ATLANTIC OCEAN

North America, 1763

N
W   E
S

SOUTH AMERICA

In CONGRESS, July 4, 1776.
The unanimous Declaration of the thirteen united States of America,

For many years, the **colonists** followed English laws. But after a while, England's laws began to anger some of the colonists. They felt English laws were unfair. And they wanted to help make any laws they had to follow. Finally, the colonists sent a Declaration of Independence to the English king. It said that a government should have the support of the people it rules. Also, the people should agree to the laws made by the government.

The Declaration of Independence also described the rights all people should have. It said all people are created equal. They have three rights that cannot be taken away. These are the right to live, the right to be free, and the right to be happy. The Declaration said that when a government takes away these rights, the people can put an end to that government and start a new one.

colonist, person who lives in a colony.

The mural above, by Chicago artist, James Bowden, was painted in honor of our country's two hundred years as an independent nation. At the left is Thomas Jefferson, author of the Declaration. In the center are some of the signers. The Liberty Bell is at the right.

189

Another part of James Bowden's mural (above) shows an important event of the American Revolution. American soldiers, led by General George Washington, won their first major battle when they slipped across the Delaware River at night to make a surprise attack on the enemy near Trenton, New Jersey.

representatives, persons chosen to act or speak for others.

The colonists fought a war with England to gain the right to rule themselves. This was the American Revolutionary War. In 1781, the colonists won the war and the right to rule themselves. The Thirteen Colonies became states. They joined together to form the United States of America.

Then they had exactly the same problem the shipwrecked islanders had. They had to decide what rules to make for themselves.

The Declaration explained what a government should be. But it didn't say how it should work. So, in 1787, **representatives** were chosen from each state to go to a meeting in Philadelphia. At the meeting, the representatives were to write a constitution, or plan of government, for our new country.

How should our laws be made? That was the first question the Constitution writers in Philadelphia faced. Think back a minute. The shipwrecked islanders all got together in a meeting to decide what their rules would be. This kind of lawmaking worked for the islanders. There weren't many of them. They lived on a small island. People in the thirteen states were spread out over 1,200 miles. There were nearly four million of them. They couldn't all get together in a meeting to decide on their laws.

The Constitution writers decided that the people from each state should choose representatives. These representatives would form a special group called Congress. Congress would make the laws.

Congress would make the laws, but who would see that the people followed them? This was the next question the Constitution writers had to answer. They decided that our country needed a leader who would make certain the laws were followed. That leader would be the President, chosen by the people from all the states.

The Constitution writers set up a third part of our government, too. It's made up of our courts and judges. They would settle arguments about what the laws mean.

Congress makes the laws.

The President sees that the laws are followed.

The courts settle arguments about the laws.

The Constitution writers divided the government into these three parts so that one part wouldn't get too strong. Suppose, for instance, the captain on the island said, "Because I am leader, I don't have to build my own house. Others will have to do it for me." The Constitution writers thought of problems like this. They hoped that if one part of government got too strong, the other parts would check or limit its power.

The Constitution writers knew that as time goes on things change. So they set up a way for the people to add changes to the Constitution. In fact, ten changes or **amendments** were added to the Constitution right away. People were worried that the new Constitution didn't spell out their rights well enough. So the first ten amendments were added to describe the rights and freedoms of the people.

Some symbols of our new nation are shown in this part of James Bowden's mural (below). Our nation's first flag in the shape of the Thirteen Colonies is at the left. Independence Hall in Philadelphia, where the Declaration and Constitution were signed, is in the center. The American eagle is at the right.

The first amendment protects people's rights to worship as they please. It also says that people have a right to get together in groups. They can speak or write about anything they want as long as they don't hurt anybody on purpose. Other amendments protect the rights of people accused of crimes. Because the first ten amendments spell out the rights of the American people, they are called the Bill of Rights.

Why were the rights described in the Bill of Rights so important to Americans? Because at times in our past, people had been without certain rights. Their experiences made them feel strongly about the rights they should have. You will read about some of these experiences in the next lesson.

Think About It
1. How can rules help people in groups?
2. Why didn't some people on the island like Russell Armstrong's rule?
3. What are colonies?
4. The Declaration of Independence explained what our government should be. Name some of the things it said.
5. What is the difference between the Declaration of Independence and the Constitution?
6. What are the three parts of our government? Why are they separate? What does each part do?
7. What are amendments?
8. What is the Bill of Rights? Why was it added to the Constitution?

The League of the Iroquois

"It would be a strange thing if six nations of Indian tribes should be able to form such a union, and be able to carry it out in such a manner that it has lasted for ages . . . and yet that a like union should be unsuitable for ten or a dozen English colonies to whom it is more necessary and must be more advantageous."

Those words were spoken by a colonial leader named Benjamin Franklin in 1750. Joined together, he felt the colonies would be strong—strong enough to defend themselves against enemies and to fight against England's unfair laws. Separate and apart, as they were in 1750, they were weak and unprotected.

At a meeting of the colonies in Albany, New York, in 1754, Franklin presented a "plan of union." According to his plan, each colony would choose representatives to a "grand council." This council would pass laws that all the colonies would follow. Where did Franklin get the idea for such a plan? Very possibly, from the Iroquois Indians.

About 200 years before the Albany meeting, the six nations of Iroquois joined together to

194

form the League of the Iroquois. The original aim of the League was to promote peace among the Iroquois. Later, joined together in the League, the Iroquois became powerful opponents in war.

Women and men played different parts in this League government. Women chose the men who were the representatives, or chiefs, from each tribe to the Great Council of the Iroquois, called the Longhouse. Women decided what would be discussed at the Great Council. Often the chief had to decide on ways to solve problems. This sometimes involved making rules for the people in all the tribes. If the chiefs did not do their jobs well, women could remove them from the Council.

Benjamin Franklin's plan of government was not accepted by the colonists at the Albany meeting in 1754. But the government of the United States that was formed thirty-three years later was like the Longhouse Council in many ways. Can you think how?

Lesson 2   Why America?

Jonathan Brewster was afraid. He didn't want to believe what he had just heard. "Father, Father," he yelled as he ran down the road to his house. "They've arrested some men, and now they might be coming for you!"

Jonathan's father, William Brewster, had feared this moment for some time. That same year two of his friends had been arrested. "Arrested," thought William. "Arrested, just because we choose to worship God our own way, instead of in the Church of England."

That was more than 300 years ago. At that time, there was only one kind of church in England. People were not allowed to worship in any other way. Some people thought this law was unfair.

One of these people was William Brewster. Brewster and others who believed as he did quietly broke away from the Church of England. They held their own secret church services. They were called Separatists because they had separated from the Church of England.

"It is clear that we will never be free to worship as we please in England," said William Brewster, "and it is dangerous to stay here any longer." So the Separatists moved to Holland, a country where all people were free to worship as they pleased. But after living in Holland a few years, they began to see that their families were becoming more Dutch than English. This worried them. They wanted to hold onto the English language and the English ways of doing things.

People in Europe had heard many stories about a new land across the sea. Some English people had already moved there. That made the Separatists hopeful. They thought, "Maybe this is the place we've been looking for, the place where our families can worship as they please and still hold onto the English ways and language."

So they sailed on the Mayflower bound for North America. They became known as Pilgrims. In 1620, they landed in what is now the state of Massachusetts.

Liberty for All?

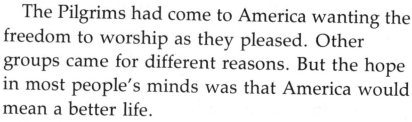

The Pilgrims had come to America wanting the freedom to worship as they pleased. Other groups came for different reasons. But the hope in most people's minds was that America would mean a better life.

Read the advertisement below. It was written in 1666 to get people to come to America. What does it promise settlers in our country?

First, There is full and free Liberty granted to all, so that no man may be questioned about his Religion; but obeying the Government, every one may worship God after their own way.

Secondly, Every Free-man and Free-woman that comes by the 25 of March next, 1667 may buy 100 Acres of Land for Himself, Wife, and Children. He may buy 100 Acres more for every Man-servant he brings to work the land, and 50 Acres for every Woman-servant and Slave.

Thirdly, Every Man-servant at the time of his freedom may buy 100 Acres of Land for Himself and Children for ever, and 50 Acres of Land for the Women-servants on the same conditions.

Those (in London) who labour (work) and can hardly earn enough to live on shall do well to go to this place (Carolina colony), where any man what-ever, who is willing to work hard, may earn a comfortable living, and be in a way to raise his fortunes far beyond what he could ever hope for in England.

The first paragraph describes freedom of religion. Besides the Pilgrims, many groups came in the hope of worshiping freely. One group was the Puritans. Instead of wanting to break away from the Church of England, the Puritans wanted to change or purify it. They felt the Church of England did not practice their religion as simply as it should.

198

So the Puritans sailed to America to find the place that offered freedom of religion. But once they started a colony in Massachusetts, they passed a law that said people could not worship in any way except the Puritan way!

One Puritan, Anne Hutchinson, formed a group to meet and talk about Puritan beliefs. During these meetings, she talked about new ways to think about the Puritan religion. Many Puritans believed that what she said went against their beliefs. They said that either she must take back things she had said or she must leave the colony.

Anne Hutchinson believed in the right to speak freely. She and her family left Massachusetts. They started a new settlement, Portsmouth, which became part of the state of Rhode Island.

Look at the ad again on page 198. It promised that in America people could own land. At that time, many people in Europe couldn't buy land even if they had the money for it. Most of the land was owned by a few wealthy families. By law, land passed from father to oldest son. Other sons without land could choose to join the army or the church. For those who chose neither, America looked good. America offered them more choices of jobs. America offered them land.

Even the poor who had no hopes of ever owning land in England could own land in America. If they couldn't pay for their trip over, others paid for it. Then they worked as servants in America until their fare was paid back. Sometimes they worked many years in this country before they became "free men." When they were free, they were allowed to own land.

At that time, owning land in America was a right for free whites only. During a certain time in our history, one large group of people was kept from owning land.

That group came to America, not because they wanted to, but because they were forced to. They were African people brought here to be the slaves of others. In a country founded on freedom for all people, they were not free. They couldn't choose their own jobs, places to live, or ways to spend their time.

Black Americans and other groups in our country had to fight for the rights and freedoms promised in the Declaration of Independence. In the next lesson, you will read about some of the women and men who worked to change things that were unfair to some people.

This painting, done in 1846, shows people being taken from Africa to be sold as slaves in America.

Think About It

1. Who were the Pilgrims? Who were the Puritans?
2. Why did Anne Hutchinson leave Massachusetts?
3. Give some reasons why different people came to this country.
4. Why were rights and freedom of choice so important to our nation's founders that they included them in the Declaration of Independence?
5. Did everybody in our country have the same rights and freedoms? Explain.

Lesson 3 Their Rights Were Earned

Frederick couldn't wait for a night when the moon was high. On nights like those he would tiptoe out of his house, a book under his arm. Then, under the light of the moon, he would study. Frederick was teaching himself to read. He didn't have much chance to learn as others his age did. Frederick was born in Maryland in 1817. He was the slave of Hugh and Sophie Auld.

Sophie Auld had taught Frederick the alphabet. She told her husband what a quick learner he was. Hugh Auld quickly ordered the lessons stopped. Like many others of his time, he believed that slaves should never learn to read. He said that if they learned to read, they'd want to be free.

Frederick had overheard what Hugh Auld had said. Now he knew that learning how to read was the most important thing he could do if he were ever to be free.

Years later in about 1830, Frederick escaped to the North where **slavery** was not allowed. He was finally free, but one thing still bothered him. He had left behind many black people who were still slaves. "I must help them win their freedom too," he thought, "but how?"

Then he learned that some people—both black and white—were forming groups to speak out against slavery. Frederick started going to the meetings. He told them how it felt to be a slave. He told his story so well that when he finished speaking, everyone stood up and cheered. Soon he was traveling all over the northern states making speeches against slavery.

But that was not enough. In 1847, he started a newspaper to tell more people about the wrongs of slavery. His paper was the voice of all black people who were still slaves, who couldn't speak out for themselves. Douglass called his paper *The North Star*, because it was the North Star in the sky that showed slaves the way to freedom in the North.

Disagreements about slavery finally led to another war in our country. It was the Civil War. The southern states wanted to keep slavery. The northern states wanted it stopped. The two sides fought, and the northern states won the war.

In 1865, a new amendment was added to the Constitution. It put an end to slavery. Later, two other amendments were added. The first gave black Americans the rights listed in the Declaration of Independence. The second gave them the right to vote.

Women had been leaders in the fight against slavery. But helping to end slavery made them realize the rights they didn't have. Two women, Lucretia Mott and Elizabeth Stanton, tried to go to the World Anti-Slavery Convention in 1840, but they were turned away at the door. Angered, they decided to hold a meeting on women's rights. Eight years later, the world's first Women's Rights Convention was held. Women from all over the country met to discuss ways for getting their rights, especially the right to vote.

Women in New York City marching for the right to vote in 1913. The amendment giving women the right to vote wasn't added to the Constitution until 1920.

Women today are fighting for another amendment to be added to the Constitution. It says that people cannot be denied equal rights because of their sex.

Women won some rights during the next eighty years. But it wasn't until 1920 that an amendment was added to the Constitution giving women the right to vote.

Today there are twenty-six amendments to the Constitution. Many of them were added to give all Americans the same rights. No doubt there will be more added.

Think About It

1. What did Frederick Douglass do to help end slavery?
2. What happened when women tried to help end slavery?
3. How did amendments help make things more fair for people in our country?
4. What rights and freedoms were promised in the Declaration of Independence? Were they true for all people?
5. Do all Americans today have the same rights and freedoms?

Lesson 4   A Nation of Immigrants

Dear Mother Elsa,

Thank you for your letter. I have been waiting to hear the news of my brother as a father. So they call my niece Veronica, not a very Swedish name! Sometimes I think about what I would call my child. It would have to be a name that is both English and Swedish. My Swedish friend, Mia, down the street recently got a girl. (It's funny that the only Swedish person I know in Cleveland should live only some houses away!) She wants to teach her daughter Swedish, but this means that she must speak Swedish all the time to the child, and that is not easy. After living here for some time, English comes to me easier than Swedish. I speak Swedish so seldom.

Just to make it clear, of course, there are other Swedes living in Cleveland. I just don't know them. I have found that most Swedish foods can be bought here. The yellow peas, herring, lingonberries, and knackebrod [knek′ə-brœd′]. Other things I have not been able to find here in Cleveland are possible to buy in Chicago.

Let me tell you a little about Andersonville, the Swedish block in Chicago. The stores have Swedish names, the things for sale are Swedish, and you can hear Swedish spoken often. There you can find the pearl-sugar and the special vinegar and Swedish Christmas decorations. A Swedish newspaper, the *Svenska* [sven′skə] *Amerikanaren Tribunen,* has its office here. But Andersonville isn't as strong a center for Swedes as it used to be. People in the United States tend to move outside the city when they can afford more expensive houses. Not as in Sweden where the best, most expensive place to live is downtown!

Last Monday I went to a neighborhood meeting. The word "neighborhood" is hard to describe. It means the area where you live. A neighborhood has stores and maybe a school for young children. Neighborhood is something that it is easy to say "my" about. That is a spot on earth that I feel I belong to.

So my neighborhood had a meeting to talk about plans for the school and for teaching white and black students together. That probably doesn't mean much to you. But in some parts of the United States blacks live mostly in one area of town and whites live mostly in another. That means that in the same city you may have schools that don't have one single black student or not one single white student. The result of this is that blacks and whites never get to know each other. And what you don't know tends to frighten you. Well, you should understand, knowing how distrustful most Swedes are toward foreigners moving to Sweden.

We are still working on our house; it definitely feels like home. For Lent I have put the colored feathers on branches, not birch branches, but they will become green anyway! Customs are important to me.

Many cars here have stickers that read, "I'd rather live in Cleveland Heights." I guess that is so for me, too. I still don't know when I will be coming to Sweden this summer.

Yours,
Kerstin

Kerstin Olofsson grew up in Sweden. Now she makes her home in the United States.

How is it Kerstin can find Swedish groceries in Cleveland, Ohio? A "little Sweden" in the middle of Chicago, Illinois? From the time of the Pilgrims to the present day, **immigrants** have poured into our land. In fact, the United States has been called a "nation of immigrants." This is because all Americans, except the American Indians, are immigrants themselves or the **descendants** of immigrants.

immigrants, people who move from one country to another.

descendants, the children, grandchildren, great-grandchildren, etc., born to a certain family or group.

The Swedish-American Museum in Andersonville. Run by volunteers in the neighborhood, the museum has exhibits dealing with the history and customs of Swedish Americans in this country.

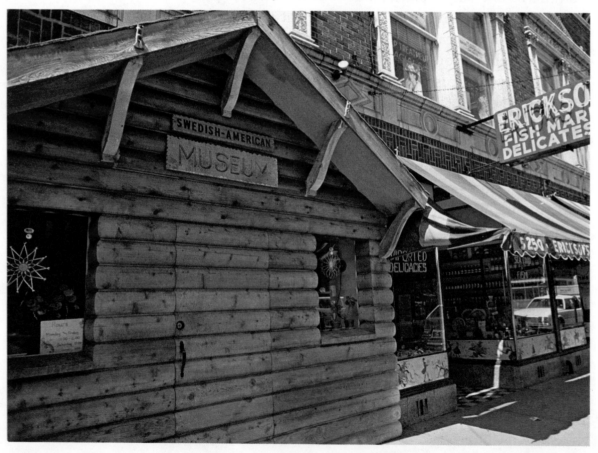

Many immigrants have come to this country looking for different kinds of freedom—to own land, to find work, to worship, to speak and write about things they cared about without fear of being punished. Once here, they found another kind of freedom, the freedom to live in the United States and still keep the **customs** of their **native** lands.

To understand why immigrants did not want to give up some of their customs, imagine you're an immigrant to a new land. You've left behind your friends, your family, everything you've ever known. But you've made up your mind to make this new land home. It will mean a better life.

You get off the airplane in your new country. Everything seems strange. You don't hear one word of your own language. With some trouble, you finally get your suitcases. Your next problem is to find the home of the relative you've never met. This person is going to help you get settled in your new country. No one understands when you try to ask directions. Finally someone understands when you write it out. She tells you how to get there by bus.

custom, habit or way of doing something that a group of people follows over a long period of time.

native, the place or country of birth.

The bus ride is the biggest problem of all. You don't know American money. You try to figure how much is needed, but the people behind you get angry that you're taking so much time.

Finally, you see the street where you're to get off the bus. You walk along and what do you see? Something like Kerstin saw in Andersonville. People selling newspapers written in your language! People speaking your language! Now you don't feel so strange and all alone.

Maybe you'll settle here for a while. Living with others who speak your language and have the same customs should make life in this strange land a little less strange.

There are other reasons why immigrants often choose to live with others from the same country. Some Americans didn't want to share this country with any new immigrants. This made it difficult for immigrants to live and work where they wanted.

Helen Wong Jean tells about some of the problems Chinese Americans faced in this country.

". . . My father came here from Canton, [a city in southern China], during the gold rush. . . . We have progressed over the years and what we had to go through! . . . At one time, you couldn't buy a house, you couldn't rent an apartment, you couldn't get a job, because you were Chinese. . . . [Today] the doors are opening for our people, more so than before."

"Doors are opening" for the Chinese and for others because many Americans now believe that differences among our people make our country better and stronger. They know that people can have pride in their past and can love this country at the same time.

Rose Toy's mother wanted her children to learn American ways and the English language. But she also wanted them to be proud of themselves and their past. Rose Toy tells how her mother kept Chinese ways alive.

Immigrants panning for gold at Auburn Ravine, California, in 1852. A war in China and news of the gold rush brought many Chinese immigrants to the United States in the 1850s.

A Chinese family in Chicago.

"We'd come home and jibber jabber [in English], do our homework, talk among ourselves, and she never knew what was going on. As long as we were doing our homework and talking among ourselves, it was all right; but as soon as we sat down at the dinner table [we had to] speak Chinese or *else*."

Think About It

1. Why do you think many immigrants chose the United States as their new home?
2. Give some reasons why immigrants often choose to live in communities with other people from the same country.
3. America has been called a "nation of immigrants." Give some personal examples of what this means.

When You Read Social Studies

Read the group of sentences below. Try to decide what's wrong with them.

First, the captain sent out a group to explore the island.

Second, the storm wrecked our ship.

Third, we arrived on the island.

What's wrong with the sentences? Why don't they make sense? If you said they don't make sense because they're not in the order in which they happened, you're right. What happened first? Second? Third?

The same is true of events in the past. Arranging them in order will help you make sense out of them. Below are some of the events you just studied. Try to place them in the order in which they happened.

1. The Pilgrims came to America to gain religious freedom.
2. Frederick Douglass started a newspaper to tell people about the wrongs of slavery.
3. The colonists fought with England and won the right to rule themselves.
4. England's laws angered some of the colonists.
5. Women won the right to vote.
6. Colonists set up their own government founded on the ideas of freedoms and rights.
7. Slavery in the United States was ended.
8. The six nations of Iroquois Indians joined together to form the League of the Iroquois.

Lesson 5   Around the World . . .

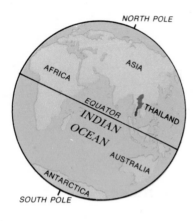

The United States is a nation of immigrants. The immigrants came from all over the world. They came from many different backgrounds. They brought with them and kept alive a variety of different customs.

Some other countries are different. They were not founded by immigrants, but are made up of people whose families have lived there for generations. They share the same backgrounds and the same customs. Thailand [tī′land] is a country like that. Let's look at some of its customs.

What happens when you greet a friend? "Hello, Tom," or "Hi, Linda," you might say. You might wave. What happens when grown-ups say "hello"? They often shake hands.

Now try this. Press your hands together. Hold them up in front of your face. Now, bow your head way down. That's how people often say "hello" in Thailand. It's called the *wai* [wī].

Now, say "hello" to Lamai [là mī′] Patibatsarakich. She lives in Thonburi [tōn′bėr′ē], a city across the river from Bangkok, the capital of Thailand. If you have trouble saying her name, you're not alone. Most people in Thailand have long last names like Lamai's. So almost everybody just goes by first names.

214

Like many in Thailand, Lamai lives on a *klong* or canal. At sunrise, the *klongs* in Thonburi come alive. Boats called *sampans* [sum′pun′] are the city's supermarkets. Loaded with rice and fruits and vegetables, the *sampans* float from door to door selling food for the day. People can buy anything they need on the *klongs*, from pots and pans to toys.

This morning Lamai's mother is busy cooking breakfast. As it happens every morning, a Buddhist monk comes to the door. Lamai's mother offers him a small bit of food.

A morning of buying and selling on a *klong* in Thonburi.

215

Children in Thailand learn to read and write English as well as Thai which has a 100-letter alphabet.

Most of the people in Thailand are Buddhists. They follow the teachings of Buddha. They believe that if they obey certain rules, they will have a good life and will be born again into a better life. Offering food every morning to Buddhist monks is one way to earn a better life.

At the age of 21, men can become Buddhist monks. Lamai's brother, Somnuk [sum nŭk′], looks forward to the day when he will shave his head and eyebrows and will put on the orange robes of Buddhist monks. Then he will have to follow strict rules. Somnuk can be a monk for a day, a few months, or for his whole lifetime. He has those choices.

Somnuk's father was a monk for a while. Now he is a boat builder farther down the *klong*. Lamai's mother and grandmother make hats all day. They sell them to Chalee [kȧ′lē], the owner of the hat and basket store.

Lamai and Somnuk are ready now to take the *sampan* to school. But first they must offer food to the *phi* [pē]. Most Thai people believe in *phis* or spirits. The *phis* live in spirit houses that to you might look like bird houses on posts. Thai people believe that, if treated kindly, the *phis* will guard the family and keep them safe.

Lamai and Somnuk like school. It is run by the government, but it is taught by Buddhist monks at religious temples. All day the children recite lessons in math, English, and Thai. At the end of the day, they paddle home.

Before entering the house, Lamai and Somnuk remove their shoes. Thais believe that wearing shoes indoors is not polite. Then the family sits down to a dinner of rice, fish, and vegetables. Before bed, Lamai's family burns candles and offers sweet smelling flowers to the *phi*, thanking it for another day of good luck and safety.

A spirit house is built in the corner of the yard so that the shadow of the main house will never fall on it and bring bad luck.

217

And Back Again

Most Thais follow the same customs as Lamai. That's because their families have lived in Thailand for generations. They share the same background.

People came to the United States from all over the world. They have many different backgrounds. For that reason, our country is made up of a variety of customs.

Now, let's go back around the world and look at another country. Be thinking as you read—is it like Thailand or is it like the United States?

Dear Roberto,

We're here. It was a long trip. The truck stopped for other families along the way. A lot more got on in Belém [bə lem′]. The truck stopped every night, but it rained so hard nobody could get out. Then we went by big cattle ranches, Roberto. The gauchos waved to us. We cooked dinner outdoors and slept on our hammocks. Did it feel good to get out of that truck!

Tell your father there *are* many jobs open in Brasilia [brə zē′lyə]. Daddy says he won't have trouble finding one. Mama has been working hard making baskets. We'll go into the city this Saturday to see if we can sell them.

Brasilia is very big, Roberto. Much bigger than Parnaiba [pàr′nə ē′və]. There are buildings that reach to the sky. Everything is so new. Some people live in

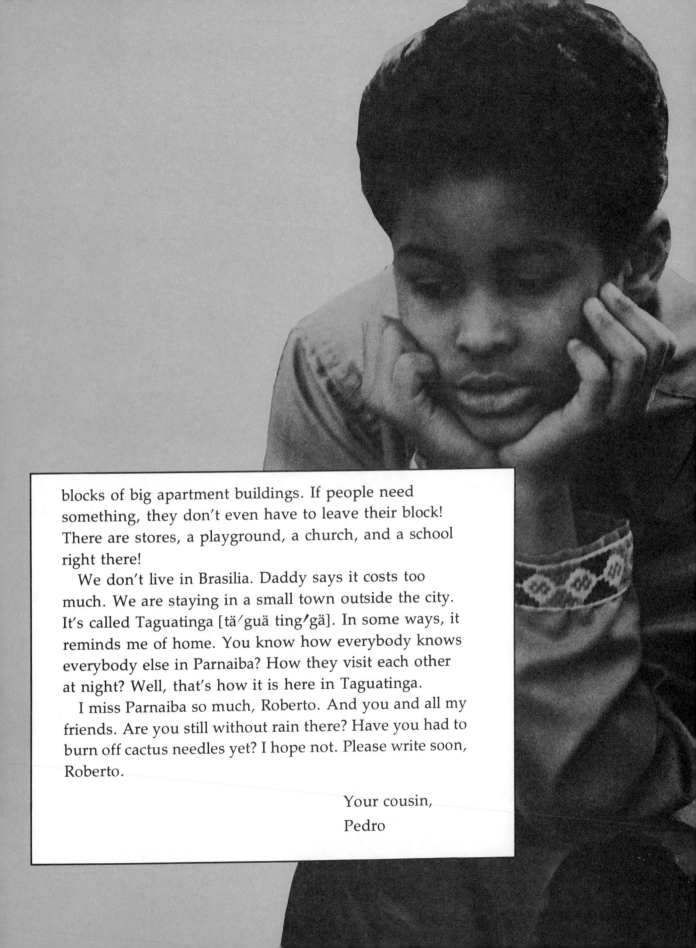

blocks of big apartment buildings. If people need
something, they don't even have to leave their block!
There are stores, a playground, a church, and a school
right there!

We don't live in Brasilia. Daddy says it costs too
much. We are staying in a small town outside the city.
It's called Taguatinga [tä⁄guä ting′gä]. In some ways, it
reminds me of home. You know how everybody knows
everybody else in Parnaiba? How they visit each other
at night? Well, that's how it is here in Taguatinga.

I miss Parnaiba so much, Roberto. And you and all my
friends. Are you still without rain there? Have you had to
burn off cactus needles yet? I hope not. Please write soon,
Roberto.

Your cousin,
Pedro

Every year Brazilians celebrate Carnival, a festival of dancing, singing, and parading that lasts for several days.

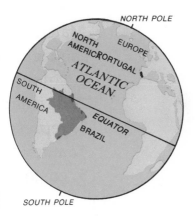

Pedro and Roberto live in Brazil, a country in South America. Find it on the globe. Brazil is like the United States, because it was settled by people from other countries. Indians were the first Brazilians. Then immigrants came from Portugal and Africa.

Brazilians today speak Portuguese. Their food can be traced back to Africa, along with some of the dances performed during Carnival time. Pedro's mother weaves baskets just as the Indians did centuries before.

Like the United States, Brazil is a mixture of customs. But the customs that Pedro and Roberto follow are different from yours. They're different from Lamai's, too. Your life would be different if you lived in Thailand or Brazil or any other country. That's because your customs decide the things you do every day. People with different customs have different choices.

Think About It

1. Describe some customs in Thailand.
2. The people in Thailand share the same background. Is that true in the United States? Explain.
3. How is Brazil like the United States?
4. Compare a day in your life with Pedro's.
5. Compare a day in your life with Lamai's.

221

What Do You Know?

Words to Know

Match the words on the left with the correct meanings on the right. Write your answers on another sheet of paper.

1. colonies
2. descendant
3. representative
4. amendments
5. custom

a. changes in the Constitution
b. persons chosen to act or speak for others
c. the children, grandchildren, great-grandchildren, etc., born to a certain family or group
d. groups of communities in one country that are ruled by another country
e. habit or way of doing something that a group of people follows over a long period of time

Ideas to Know

Number a paper from 1 to 9. Write the word next to the number that completes the sentences below.

__(1)__ are rules made by governments that all the people must follow. The basic laws of our country and plan for our government are contained in the __(2)__. It says that __(3)__ chosen from each state form a group to make our laws. This group is called __(4)__. The other two parts of our country's government are __(5)__ and the __(6)__. Our government is divided into these three parts so that one part doesn't get too __(7)__. The first __(8)__ amendments to our Constitution, called the __(9)__ _____ _____, describe the rights of the people.

222

Using What You Know

The Brewsters	Helen Wong Jean
Frederick Douglass	The Puritans

Listed above are some immigrants or descendants of immigrants to our country. Immigrants are people who move from one country to another. For each of those above, list the place from which they or their ancestors immigrated. Locate the places on a globe. Then list the reasons why each person or group came. How are the reasons alike? How are they different?

It might help you to compare the reasons why people came to this country if you put your information in chart form. See the example below.

Person or Group	Place they or their ancestors came from	Reasons why they came
1.	1.	1.
2.	2.	2.
3.	3.	3.
4.	4.	4.

Unit 7 Your Changing Community

224

Lesson 1 The Sleeping Dragon

Flat yellow grasslands. Endless grasslands. You've been driving west forever, and you've seen nothing but these flat golden fields. Then suddenly you see something up ahead. What is it? The ridged back of a sleeping dragon? No, it's a mountain! Jutting right out of the flatness, stretching up out of its own **foothills.** Below it, snuggled into the space where the grasslands meet the mountain, is the community of Boulder, Colorado.

That dragon-shaped mountain is what visitors remember most about Boulder. It's what the people who live there love best. They've seen their mountain change in the different lights of the day, in all the different seasons. They've seen its jagged ridges glow pink in the first light of morning. They've seen them silver with frost and dusted with snow.

What a thrill, you think, to be able to look up from anywhere in town and see that sleeping monster. But the view in Boulder is changing. From some places in town, what used to be a view of the dragon mountain and the snowcapped mountains behind it is now a view of rooftops and the towers of hotels and apartment buildings.

foothills, low hills at the base of a mountain range.

The reason for the spread of rooftops? People and more people. In the last fifteen years, Boulder has grown from a middle-sized town of 20,000 people to a city of nearly 100,000. And it's not just Boulder. Other cities are growing, too. They're growing because some cities in our country are shrinking. People are on the move. Look at the map. Can you tell which way they're moving? If you said from the northern part of our country to the southern part, you were right. Here's why.

In recent years, costs have gone up a lot in the northern and eastern parts of our country. That caused many large businesses to move to cities in the southern and western parts of our country where costs were not so high. Businesses hire a lot of people. People tend to move where jobs are. This is part of the reason for Boulder's growth. One big company moved to Boulder. Hundreds of people followed.

But jobs aren't the only reason people move. Some people moved to Boulder and other small cities in the South and Southwest just to get out of the big, crowded cities. They wanted out of traffic jams, concrete neighborhoods, crime, and wall-to-wall people. The South and Southwest offered open space and beautiful natural surroundings, new experiences for some city **dwellers.**

dwellers, persons who live in a certain place.

America's Fastest Growing Cities*

1. Huntington Beach, California
2. Colorado Springs, Colorado
3. Anchorage, Alaska
4. Virginia Beach, Virginia
5. San Jose, California
6. El Paso, Texas
7. Austin, Texas
8. Anaheim, California
9. Las Vegas, Nevada
10. Albuquerque, New Mexico
11. Phoenix, Arizona
12. Honolulu, Hawaii
13. San Diego, California
14. San Antonio, Texas
15. Miami, Florida
   * Cities over 100,000

America's Fastest Shrinking Cities*

1. Dayton, Ohio
2. St. Louis, Missouri
3. Cleveland, Ohio
4. Minneapolis, Minnesota
5. Buffalo, New York
6. Atlanta, Georgia
7. Detroit, Michigan
8. Pittsburgh, Pennsylvania
9. Newark, New Jersey
10. Gary, Indiana
11. Cincinnati, Ohio
12. Fort Worth, Texas
13. Seattle, Washington
14. Chicago, Illinois
15. Milwaukee, Wisconsin
   * Cities over 100,000

But rapid, unplanned growth causes problems. Cities have a hard time keeping up. The more people, the more things cities need. Houses are needed fast. So are roads, schools, stores, sewers. Builders build quickly to meet these needs. They tend to use the space surrounding the city because it's the quickest and easiest way to build. Often they build more houses than are needed. The empty houses draw even more people to the area.

This all began to happen in Boulder. The sea of rooftops spread out onto the grasslands and up into the foothills. Four-lane highways cut through town where two lanes went before. Shopping centers and fast food chains multiplied. More businesses, more restaurants, more areas of open land covered with houses and apartment buildings. The mountains were in danger and so was the beauty.

The people of Boulder decided that something had to be done. They made some decisions to save their city's beauty and space.

Think About It
1. Tell how Boulder, Colorado, has changed in the last fifteen years.
2. Which parts of the United States are growing? Give reasons for this growth.
3. What can happen when a city grows very quickly?
4. Why are the people in Boulder worried?

231

THE JOB OF AN

How to save the natural beauty of their community. How to slow down uncontrolled growth. The people of Boulder had to decide. But decisions like these take thought and planning. Most cities hire specially trained people called urban planners to help them with these decisions.

In any city, urban planners have many jobs to do. They draw up plans for guiding the growth of their city. They judge how land can best be used. Would it be better to build here or there? Would it be better to recycle an old building or to tear it down and build a new one? They predict growth. They study city services like the police department and transportation system. They decide if these services can meet people's needs if and when the city grows. If they can't, the urban planners must design programs for updating the services.

URBAN PLANNER

It's also the urban planners' job to keep their city pleasant and livable. They decide how to make a residential area nicer or a business district more attractive. They help fight pollution and see that parks and playgrounds stay clean and usable.

A person must have many years of schooling to become an urban planner. In some cities, urban planners must pass a difficult test to qualify for the job. Urban planners must be skilled at mapmaking and must be able to figure the costs of any program they suggest.

Urban planners have to look into the future to foresee problems. Urban planners try to solve a city's problems before they happen. Think again about Boulder. What kinds of problems would urban planners face there? List some of them, then choose one and pretend you're an urban planner. How would you solve it?

Lesson 2   Choices for the Future

boom, rapid growth in business, building, and prices.

real estate, land and buildings, property.

Most of the people of Boulder wanted to protect the natural beauty of their city. But they were divided on how it should be done. Some people thought growth should be stopped, period, right now. Others disagreed. They said this was like saying, "I've got my sandbox, now you find yours someplace else." They said that people who were worried about the bad effects of growth on Boulder should think of the ways growth had been good for Boulder.

After all, Boulder was **booming.** Stores had more business. So did builders and **real estate** companies. The city of Boulder itself made good use of the extra money that was collected in the form of taxes. Now Boulder could repair cracked sidewalks. It could fix up some of those forgotten parks.

The problem then was how to protect Boulder's beauty without hurting its pocketbook too much. In 1971, the people decided to vote.

Should there be a limit on how many people could live in Boulder? The people voted "no" to that. But they voted "yes" to slow down the growth. That meant the city council could draw up plans for guiding growth, but not for limiting growth.

One plan the people of Boulder had already voted "yes" to was the Greenbelt Plan. It was a plan for guiding the growth so that Boulder's beauty would not be spoiled.

The plan drew an imaginary belt around Boulder. The belt was land that didn't have houses on it. Now it was land where houses could never be built. That meant that the sea of rooftops would never spread any farther out onto the grasslands or up the sides of the mountains.

(Bottom) Apartment buildings for college students block the view of the mountains behind Boulder. (Below) A greenbelt area around Boulder.

Another important part of Boulder's beauty is the view of the dragon-shaped mountain and the snowcaps behind it. But the view was slowly being blocked by each tall building going up. So, Boulder's city council made a rule that said buildings couldn't be built above a certain height.

The Greenbelt Plan and the building height limit were fine for seeing that Boulder stayed beautiful, that it didn't grow up or out. But Boulder was still growing, and builders were still trying to beat the rush. Houses were still going up fast all over town even if there were no people for them yet. What was to be done about slowing down growth?

Boulder's city council debates plans for limiting the city's growth.

The city council came up with another plan. It said that only 450 buildings housing four or more families could be built a year. People wanting to build this kind of housing would have to have their plans approved by a group of judges. Only the best 450 would be built.

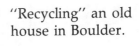
"Recycling" an old house in Boulder.

There were problems with the plan. Many worried that limiting the number of new buildings that could be built would drive up the cost of housing all over town. But in spite of these worries, the people voted "yes." The plan was accepted.

Now what? If Boulder couldn't grow up or out, where would it grow? Boulder encouraged builders to "rebuild," to **recycle** the old. That not only held down growth, but it made sure Boulder's history stayed alive. Old homes that were built 100 years ago were being repainted, repaired. The idea caught on. Recycling of homes led to recycling of buildings and businesses. "Urbanize, not suburbanize" became Boulder's new motto. Instead of building more shopping centers, one after the other making the city bigger and bigger, Boulder would rebuild its downtown. And that's exactly what it did on Pearl Street.

recycle, treat something so it can be used again.

The construction of the Pearl Street mall made this historic area once again the heart of Boulder.

attitude, way a person feels toward something.

Pearl Street is the main street of Boulder's downtown, built in the days of cowboys and gold miners. But with shiny new shopping centers springing up in other parts of town, Pearl Street had been overlooked. Its buildings, old anyway, had been left to grow older. Businesses and shoppers preferred the newness of shopping centers.

When **attitudes** changed, Pearl Street changed. Builders turned it into a beautiful, four-block shopping mall closed to cars. Now, on a summer Saturday people come to be entertained by magicians, musicians, and jugglers. Playgrounds, pools, and popcorn vendors—they are all the new Pearl Street. And Pearl Street is once again the real heart of an old-new Boulder.

The decisions the people of Boulder faced are not unusual. People in communities around the country are facing similar choices.

Jobs or nature. That's the choice facing Youngstown, Ohio. A steel company, the biggest **employer** in town, plans to shut down. For years, it has been polluting the nearby Mahoning River. Now, by law, the company must cut down on what it dumps into the water. The company feels it cannot afford the added costs of doing this.

One group of people in this community is happy the plant is closing. They say that the polluted river is an eyesore. They also claim it is a health threat to the community. For years, the people have used the water. But now the river is dead, unfit for life or use.

But some workers at the plant are angry and worried. They will be out of work. They will be faced with supporting their families until other jobs are found. Some may even have to leave Youngstown to look for work elsewhere. And what of the community itself? People without jobs will have less money to spend. That will hurt stores and businesses. The town government will be without tax dollars it collected from the steel company. Fewer taxes mean fewer city services.

Youngstown will be hurt because it has depended on the steel company and all its workers. Just as Boulder boomed when it grew, this city may suffer if it shrinks.

employer, person or company that gives work and pay to others.

Musicians entertain passers-by on the Pearl Street mall.

239

Scenic Eastport, Maine, is the home of another argument about the environment. An oil company wants to build a **refinery** there. Some groups in the community are trying to stop this. They say the refinery will spoil the clean air, the water, and the natural beauty of Eastport. Others add that if the scenery is spoiled their tourist business will be, too. And if the water turns foul, the fishing industry will be hurt.

But others say the refinery will mean jobs. And many, many people are out of work in Eastport. They also point out that the plant will help supply our country's **energy** needs.

refinery, factory that purifies something before it can be used.

energy, power.

Making choices is very difficult in all these communities. But it takes people to make choices. You are part of those people. If you think it will be a long time before you can affect decision-making in your community, read the next lesson.

Think About It

1. Why did the people of Boulder disagree on how to protect the natural beauty of their city?
2. Name some ways growth was good for Boulder.
3. What is the Greenbelt Plan?
4. What are some problems with the plan to limit house building?
5. Explain the phrase "urbanize, not suburbanize." Tell why it is important in Boulder.
6. Give reasons why the steel company in Youngstown should shut down, why it shouldn't.
7. How do people in Eastport earn their living? Will the refinery change that? How?

Lesson 3 "Save the Park!"

A group of children in Westerville, Ohio, helped save a park in their community. Happy Bee, from *Ranger Rick's Nature Magazine*, tells the story.

One day as I was flying over Westerville I saw a small pond bordered by cattails and other water plants. . . . I had come a long way, and it was a perfect place to rest.

Then I saw a group of kids talking with a man. I flew down to listen.

"Boy," one of the kids said, "I'm glad the city didn't destroy the park like they said they were going to."

"So am I," the man said. "You children saved it and should feel very proud."

How did the children save it? I asked the man, Edwin J. Gossett, to tell me the story.

"Well, Happy Bee, for years the school children have used Boyer Park to study nature. It's a wonderful outdoor **laboratory.**

laboratory, place where scientific work is done.

"Then the city decided to build a new sewer line right through the park. The builders would have to cut down many trees and dig a deep, wide trench a few feet from the pond. The kids and their teacher were afraid the water would drain away.

"They discussed the plans and what might happen. The children decided the construction would destroy the park. They didn't want that to happen.

"The kids agreed to write letters to all the city officials asking them not to harm the park. They also wrote letters to the newspaper. The editor published some of them.

"Then the kids made signs saying SAVE BOYER PARK, which they put in store windows. Because of them the grownups also became very interested in saving the park.

"When the city officials learned that the adults wanted to protect the park too, they agreed that they had to find a new route for the sewer.

"But the battle to save the park wasn't over. The city didn't have enough money to buy the land needed for the new route.

"That was when the children decided to raise as much money as they could and give it to the city. They worked very hard. They held car washes and bake sales. They went from house to house in their neighborhoods, asking people to give money for the land. They held bike marathons and sold balloons at the 4th of July parade. They raised over $800! It wasn't enough but it was a really good start.

"Later the city got the rest of the money they needed. The park was saved.

"So you see, Happy Bee, it is possible for children to help save nature."

You can help make choices in your community, too. But often the choices are difficult to make. That's because important human needs sometimes work against each other. Jobs. Energy to heat and light our homes and run our factories. Clean air, water, and natural beauty for ourselves and future generations.

This is how it often is in decision-making—having to choose among things that seem equally important. You can't avoid difficult choices in your life. What you can avoid is making thoughtless and uninformed choices. That's why it's important to find out the costs and consequences of all the courses of action open to you. This means keeping an open mind and listening to people on all sides of a problem. In the end, your choices will be influenced by your feelings and experiences and by the rules and values of your family, community, and country. But your decision will also be based on your own, valuable knowledge.

Think About It

1. What change was about to take place in Westerville, Ohio?
2. The community had several choices. What were they?
3. How did the children influence the choice that the community made?
4. What work did the children do to help bring about this change in the community?
5. How can you help change your community?
6. Think about some difficult decisions you have faced? How did you make your choice?

245

The EPA

You've just read about how growth was spoiling the natural beauty of Boulder. How a steel company in Ohio endangered life in and around the Mahoning River. In these two cases the environment was in trouble and in need of protection.

The police department in your community protects you from harm. But is there a police department to protect the environment from harm? There is now. It's called the Environmental Protection Agency or EPA for short. It was started in 1970 to protect the environment so that you and future generations of Americans can enjoy it as much as possible.

The EPA set up offices all around the country to get closer to each environmental problem as it happened. It suggested newer, stronger laws to keep the environment safe. It checked to make sure the laws were followed.

Look around you. Can you find any clues that tell you the EPA is at work?

When You Read Social Studies

The EPA may not be involved in *every* step that's taken to protect the environment. But its work has encouraged others to help. Communities and individuals everywhere have joined nature's police force.

What's been done in your community, do you know? You can find out. And it'll be easy and fun. Take a field trip. Walk or ride your bike around town. Keep your eyes and ears open, and you'll be surprised what you can learn.

Try this. As you tour your community, make a list (oh yes, it's always a good idea to carry a pencil and pad when you're a scientific scout) of all the signs you can find that have to do with protecting the environment. Remember, there are signs everywhere—on buildings, on garbage cans, even on the sides of buses and taxis.

As you ride, start a second list, or take a second field trip. This time list all the places or situations where there aren't signs but should be. All the places where the environment is in danger and could be helped.

What did you find out? Is your community doing more or less than you thought? How can you help?

What Do You Know?

Words to Know

Match the words on the left with the correct meanings on the right. Write your answers on another sheet of paper.

1. boom

2. employer

3. real estate

4. recycle

a. person or company that gives work and pay to others

b. treat something so it can be used again

c. rapid growth in business, building, and prices

d. land and buildings, property

Ideas to Know

Who might have made the following statements? On a separate piece of paper, number from one to seven. After each number, write "B" if you think someone from Boulder might have said it. Write "Y" for someone from Youngstown. Write "E" for someone from Eastport, "W" for someone from Westerville.

1. "There are so many more people in town these days that the traffic has gotten awful."

2. "The history of the oldest street in town has been kept alive in a beautiful, useful way."

3. "I'm afraid our tourist business will be hurt if there is a chance the water might become polluted."

4. "It will take some time before the river is clean and usable again."

5. "The children worked very hard to save something that was important to them and to the community."
6. "I'd like to see the refinery built. It will mean more jobs for people."
7. "We may have to move. I won't find a job here better than the one I had at the steel company."

Using What You Know
1. Take a walk around your community. Make a list of the changes that are taking place. What effect does each have on the environment?
2. Look in your local newspaper for proposed changes in your community. Make a list of them. They might include such things as the building of a new school or hospital, a new highway, a new area of houses, or a new shopping center.
3. Pick one of the proposed changes and answer these questions:
   a. What good things will happen if this change takes place?
   b. What problems might this cause for some people within the community?
   c. What could your community do if it didn't make this change?
   d. If you were a city official, would you vote for this change? Why or why not?

Handbook of Skills and Information

Getting New Information

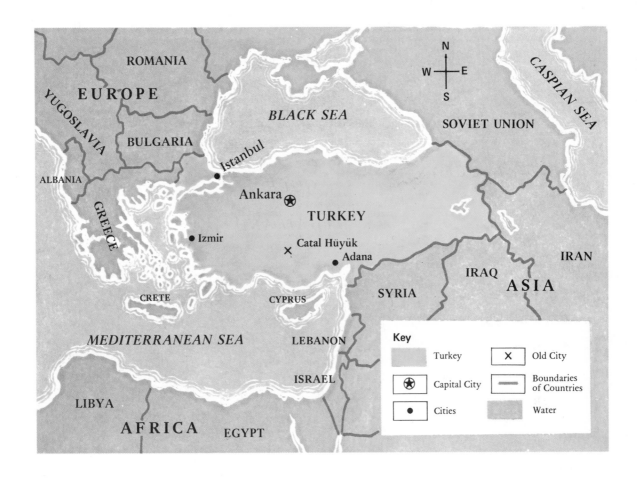

Do you remember reading about Catal Hüyük? It is one of the world's oldest cities. Its remains can be seen in Turkey.

This country lies at the eastern end of the Mediterranean Sea. Turkey is bordered by two other seas. What are their names?

Turkey joins two continents. The western part of Turkey is in Europe. The eastern part of Turkey is in Asia. What Turkish city is in Europe? Name some Turkish cities in Asia. Where is the capital?

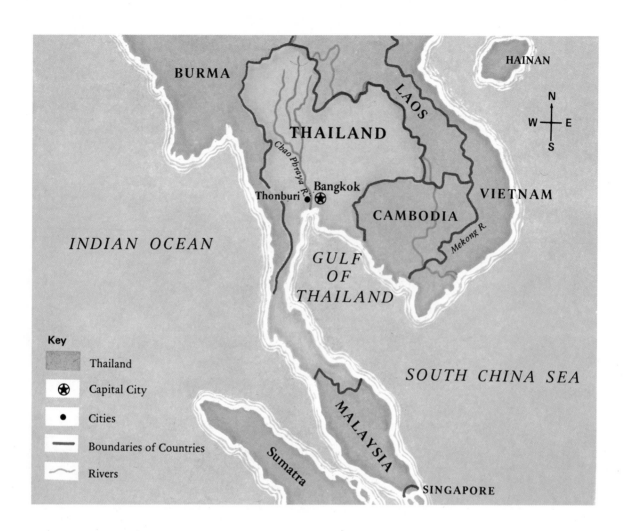

Do you remember reading about Lamai Patibatsarakich? She lives in Thailand. It is a country in Southeast Asia.

Find Thailand on the map. Read the map key to find the symbol for boundaries of countries. Thailand's neighbor to the south is Malaysia. What is Thailand's neighbor to the west? What are its neighbors to the east?

Lamai lives in the city of Thonburi. On what river is it located? Is Thonburi near the capital city of Thailand?

252

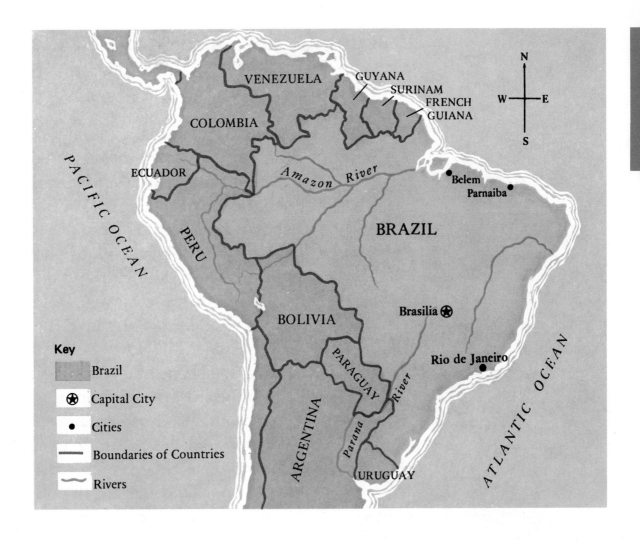

Do you remember reading about Roberto and
Pedro? They live in Brazil. It is the biggest
country in South America.

Find Brazil on the map. What large river
flows through the northern part of the country?
Into what ocean does the river flow?

Brazil is bordered on the east by the Atlantic
Ocean. The country has many, many neighbors.
What are their names?

Read the map key to find the symbol for
capital city. What is the capital of Brazil?

Practicing Map and Globe Skills

Which Way?

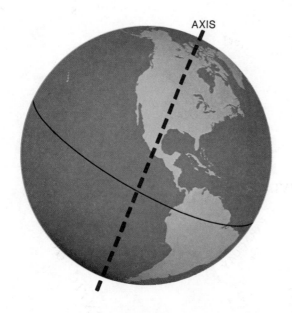

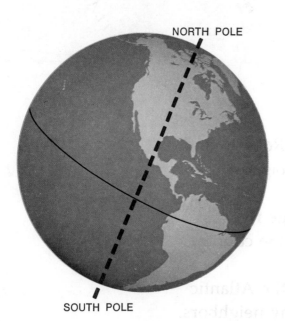

The Earth turns, or rotates, all the time. To rotate means to turn around on an axis. No one can see the Earth's axis, but it can be shown by a line. The broken line on the picture of the globe shows the location of the Earth's axis.

One end of the Earth's axis is called the North Pole. Like the Earth's axis, the North Pole cannot be seen. The North Pole can be represented by a dot.

The other end of the Earth's axis is called the South Pole. The South Pole can be represented by a dot, too. Find the North and South poles in the picture of the globe.

Direction is a word that means the way you can face or point or go. North is a direction. The word *north* means toward the North Pole. If you are going north, you are going toward the North Pole.

What does the word *south* mean? If you are going south, which pole do you reach? Do you live nearer the North Pole or the South Pole?

The North Pole is the place on Earth that is the farthest north. The South Pole is the place that is farthest south. All directions on Earth are figured from these two points.

As you read, the Earth rotates on its axis. The Earth makes one full turn each day. Toward what direction does the Earth rotate?

East is a very old word that means morning. When you look toward the direction where you see the early morning sun, you are looking east. When you are facing east, you are looking in the direction toward which the Earth is turning. See how the Earth rotates in the picture of the turning globe.

After noontime, the Earth turns you away from the sun. In the late afternoon, the sun looks as if it is low in the sky. When you look at the sun just before night comes, you are looking west.

When you face north, east is to your right, and west is to your left. If you face south, is east to your right or to your left? Is west to your right or to your left?

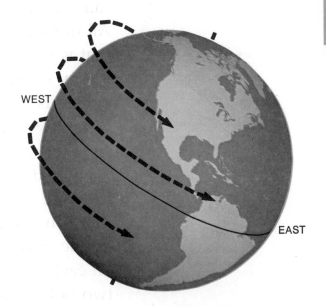

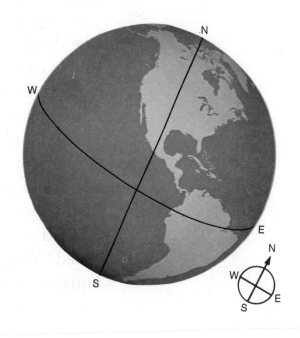

255

What Is a Hemisphere?

A ball, a grapefruit, and an orange have the same shape. All of them are round like balls. All of them are spheres. A sphere is something that is round like a ball.

Any sphere can be cut into two parts. When a sphere is cut in half, each part is the same size. When two parts are the same size, the parts are equal in size.

Look at the drawings of the globes on the opposite page. A globe is a sphere, too. Lines that run from the North Pole to the South Pole can be drawn on the globe. A dot can be placed on each north-south line, halfway between the two poles. Each dot divides its line into two equal parts.

A line can be drawn through all the dots. The line divides the globe into two equal parts. The line is called the Equator.

Earth is a sphere. It can be divided into two equal parts. Half of a sphere is called a hemisphere.

The North Pole is in the hemisphere north of the Equator. The South Pole is in the hemisphere south of the Equator. What do you think the hemisphere north of the Equator is called? What is the hemisphere south of the Equator called?

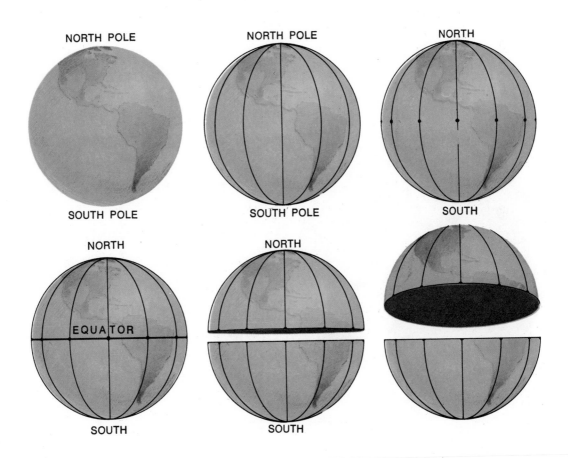

257

Here is a picture of part of the Northern Hemisphere. The continent of North America is in the Northern Hemisphere. A part of the continent of South America is also in the Northern Hemisphere. Do you live in the Northern Hemisphere?

Here is another picture of the Northern Hemisphere. You can see the symbol which stands for the North Pole. You can see parts of several continents. Can you name them? You can see where the Arctic Ocean and parts of two other oceans are located. What are their names? Where is the Equator in this picture of a globe?

Here is a picture of part of the Southern Hemisphere. Most of the continent of South America is in the Southern Hemisphere. Parts of two oceans are in the Southern Hemisphere. Look again at the globes on page 258. Are parts of these same two oceans also in the Northern Hemisphere?

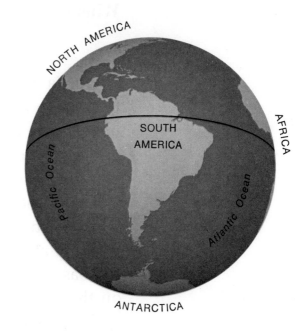

Here is another picture of the Southern Hemisphere. You can see the symbol which stands for the South Pole. What continents do you see? Which ones are in the Southern Hemisphere? You can see parts of three oceans. What are their names?

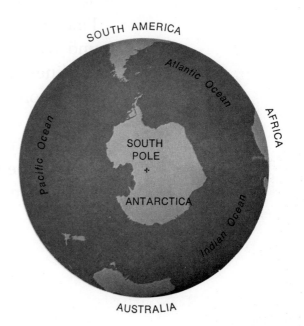

Now look at all four globes. Is there more land or water on Earth? Is most of the land on Earth north or south of the Equator?

Where Is It?

This is a map of a part of a city. Blue lines have been added to the map. Some of these lines go from west to east. These lines have numbers. Some of these lines go from north to south. These lines have letters.

If you know the number of one line and the letter of another, you can tell where a building is. Look at the map key. Find the symbol for the baseball park. Then find the baseball park on the map.

If you wanted to tell someone where the baseball park is on the map, how would the lines help you? The baseball park is found where line F and line 3 cross, at F-3.

Find the library on the map. The library is found where line D and line 1 cross, at D-1. If these lines were not on the map, how would you tell someone where the library is?

Find the college on the map. Use the lines to tell where the college is located. Find the court house on the map. Where is the court house? Find the dam on the map. Where is the dam located?

MAP OF CITY

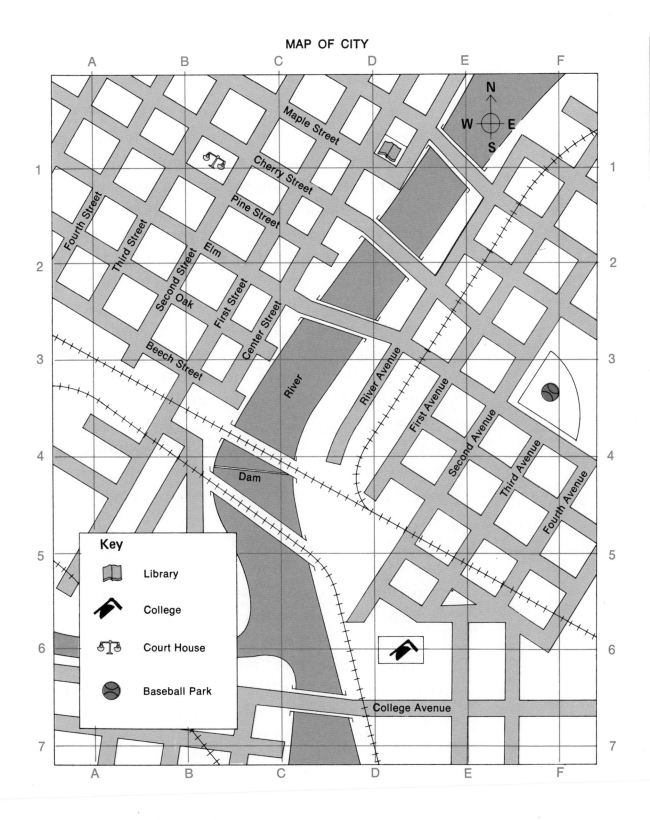

Key

- 📖 Library
- College
- ⚖ Court House
- ⚾ Baseball Park

What Is It Near?

You live in the United States of America. Your country has fifty states. What is the name of your state? Find it on the map.

The map shows the capital of your country. What is its name? The map also shows the capital of each state. What is the capital of your state? The map also shows some of the large cities in your country. Name some of them. Are there any large cities in your state?

Every state and city has its own location. Some places are near oceans. Places that have an ocean along one or more sides have coastal locations. Florida has a coastal location on the Atlantic Ocean. Oregon has a coastal location of the Pacific Ocean. Name some other states and cities with coastal locations.

Other places are far from oceans. Places that are not near oceans have interior locations. Iowa has an interior location. The city of St. Louis has an interior location. Name some other states and cities with interior location. Does your state have a coastal or an interior location?

Each place also has a location that can be described by its direction from another place. Arkansas is south of Missouri. In what direction is Colorado from Texas? Using directions, describe the location of your state capital.

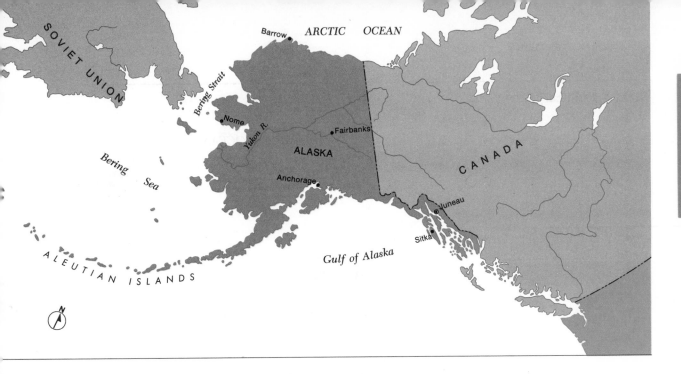

ARCTIC OCEAN

Barrow

SOVIET UNION

Bering Strait

Nome

Yukon R.

Fairbanks

ALASKA

CANADA

Bering Sea

Anchorage

Juneau

Aleutian Islands

Sitka

Gulf of Alaska

N

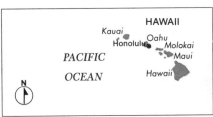

HAWAII

Kauai

Oahu
Honolulu   Molokai
            Maui

PACIFIC

OCEAN   Hawaii

N

The 50 United States

Key

★ National capital

⊙ State capital

• Large cities

‑‑‑‑ National boundary

‑‑‑‑ State boundary

Scale

| 0 | 200 | 400 Miles |

| 0 | 200 | 400 | Kilometers |

CANADA

WASHINGTON

Olympia

Salem

OREGON

MONTANA

Helena

Missouri R.

NORTH
DAKOTA

Bismarck

MINN.

MICHIGAN

MAINE

Augusta

IDAHO

Boise

Columbia R.

WYOMING

SOUTH
DAKOTA

Pierre

Minneapolis

St. Paul

WISCONSIN

Madison

Lansing

Detroit

Montpelier

VT. N.H.

Concord

NEW YORK

Albany

MASS.

Boston

Providence

Hartford

CONN. R.I.

NEVADA

Carson City

Sacramento

San Francisco

Salt
Lake
City

UTAH

Cheyenne

Platte R.

NEBRASKA

Lincoln

IOWA

Des
Moines

Chicago

ILL.

IND.

OHIO

Columbus

PA.

Pittsburgh

Harrisburg

N.J.

New York

Trenton

Philadelphia

Dover DEL.

CALIFORNIA

Los Angeles

Denver

COLORADO

Colorado R.

Arkansas R.

Topeka

KANSAS

Springfield

St. Louis

Jefferson
City

Indianapolis

Ohio R.

Frankfort

W. VA.

Charleston

Washington D.C.

Annapolis

Baltimore

MD.

Richmond

KENTUCKY

VIRGINIA

Santa Fe

ARIZONA

NEW MEXICO

Phoenix

Oklahoma
City

Red R.

OKLAHOMA

ARKANSAS

Little
Rock

MISSOURI

TENNESSEE

Nashville

Tennessee R.

NORTH
CAROLINA

Raleigh

Columbia

SOUTH CAROLINA

Dallas

TEXAS

Mississippi R.

LA.

Jackson

MISS.

ALABAMA

Atlanta

GEORGIA

Montgomery

Austin

Baton
Rouge

Houston

New Orleans

Tallahassee

FLORIDA

San
Antonio

Rio Grande

PACIFIC
OCEAN

Gulf of California

MEXICO

Gulf of Mexico

ATLANTIC
OCEAN

Miami

N

263

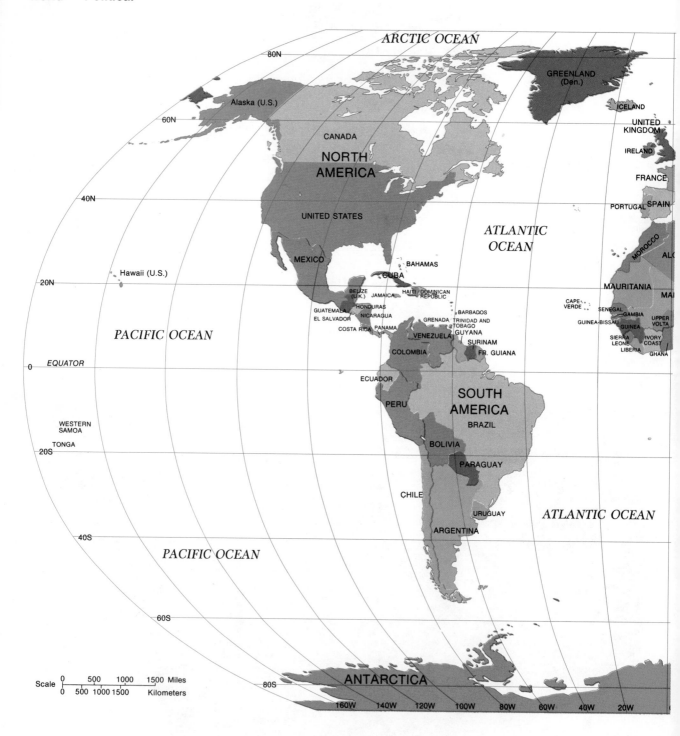

ARCTIC OCEAN

80N

GREENLAND
(Den.)

Alaska (U.S.)

ICELAND

60N

UNITED
KINGDOM

CANADA

IRELAND

NORTH
AMERICA

FRANCE

40N

ATLANTIC
OCEAN

PORTUGAL SPAIN

UNITED STATES

MOROCCO

AL

MEXICO

BAHAMAS

MAURITANIA

20N

Hawaii (U.S.)

CUBA

MAI

BELIZE
(U.K.)

HAITI DOMINICAN
REPUBLIC

CAPE
VERDE

JAMAICA

SENEGAL

GUATEMALA

HONDURAS

BARBADOS

GAMBIA

UPPER
VOLTA

EL SALVADOR

NICARAGUA

GRENADA

TRINIDAD AND
TOBAGO

GUINEA-BISSAU

GUINEA

COSTA RICA

PANAMA

GUYANA

SIERRA
LEONE

IVORY
COAST

PACIFIC OCEAN

VENEZUELA

SURINAM

LIBERIA

COLOMBIA

FR. GUIANA

GHANA

EQUATOR

0

ECUADOR

SOUTH
AMERICA

PERU

BRAZIL

WESTERN
SAMOA

BOLIVIA

TONGA

20S

PARAGUAY

CHILE

ATLANTIC OCEAN

URUGUAY

ARGENTINA

40S

PACIFIC OCEAN

60S

Scale
0   500   1000   1500 Miles
0   500 1000 1500   Kilometers

80S

ANTARCTICA

160W   140W   120W   100W   80W   60W   40W   20W

ARCTIC OCEAN

80N

NORWAY
SWEDEN
FINLAND

DENMARK
THERLANDS
EAST
GERMANY
EUROPE
WEST
LUX. GERMANY
BELGIUM
WITZERLAND
ITALY
YUGOSLAVIA
POLAND
CZECHOSLOVAKIA
AUSTRIA
HUNGARY
ROMANIA
BULGARIA

60N

UNION OF SOVIET SOCIALIST REPUBLICS
(SOVIET UNION)
ASIA

MONGOLIA

N. KOREA

40N

ALBANIA
GREECE
TURKEY

MALTA
TUNISIA
CYPRUS
LEBANON
ISRAEL
SYRIA
IRAQ
IRAN
AFGHANISTAN
JORDAN
KUWAIT
PAKISTAN

PEOPLE'S REPUBLIC
OF CHINA

S. KOREA
JAPAN

PACIFIC OCEAN

ERIA
LIBYA
EGYPT
SAUDI
ARABIA
BAHRAIN
QATAR
UNITED ARAB
EMIRATES
OMAN
NEPAL
BHUTAN
BANGLADESH
BURMA
LAO
PEOPLE'S
REPUBLIC
TAIWAN

20N

NIGER
CHAD
AFRICA
NIGERIA
SUDAN
P.D.R.
OF YEMEN
YEMEN
DJIBOUTI
INDIA
THAILAND
CAMBODIA
VIETNAM
PHILIPPINES

BENIN
CENTRAL
AFRICAN EMPIRE
CAMEROON
ETHIOPIA
SOMALIA
SRI
LANKA
BRUNEI (Br.)

OGO
QUATORIAL
GUINEA
O TOME
AND
RINCIPE
GABON
UGANDA
KENYA
MALDIVES
MALAYSIA
SINGAPORE

EQUATOR
NAURU
0

CONGO
ZAIRE
RWANDA
BURUNDI
TANZANIA
SEYCHELLES
INDIAN
OCEAN
INDONESIA
PAPUA
NEW GUINEA

CABINDA
(ANGOLA)

ANGOLA
ZAMBIA
MALAWI
COMOROS
FIJI

NAMIBIA
(SOUTH-WEST
AFRICA)
RHODESIA
BOTSWANA
MOZAMBIQUE
MADAGASCAR
MAURITIUS
20S

AUSTRALIA

SWAZILAND
SOUTH
AFRICA
LESOTHO

40S

NEW
ZEALAND

60S

ANTARCTICA

80S

20E 40E 60E 80E 100E 120E 140E 160E

Getting Ready for Standardized Tests

Every once in a while—perhaps every year or every other year—most students take a special test called a standardized achievement test. Some people call these tests by another name, like "the Iowas," "the Metro," "the Stanford," "the SRA tests," etc. The tests are printed in separate booklets. The teacher reads special directions from a teacher's manual. Usually you "color" in ovals or circles to show your answer choices. Sometimes you do this right in your test booklet, but often you show your answer choices on a separate answer sheet. The schedule for the whole school may be changed to give the tests to everyone at the same time. No matter how these tests are given in your school, you should try to do your best.

1. Work through each section of the test as quickly as you can. Do not spend a lot of time on a question that you cannot answer. If there is time left over, then you can go back and try to answer those questions you skipped.

2. Always be sure that the question number and the number of your answer are the same. If you get mixed up, quickly go back to straighten it out. Erase completely, and mark your answers in the proper place.

3. Do not be concerned if you cannot answer all questions. The tests are made difficult on purpose.

4. If you are not sure of an answer, it is wise to guess.

5. Above all, try not to be nervous or upset by the standardized tests. You will probably take many of them throughout your school years. They are a good way to find out what you already know and what you still need to learn.

On the next few pages are several varieties of sample tests made to look like the real ones. The questions are taken from the material in this book, however. You can use them to get acquainted with standardized tests, and to practice taking them. Write your answers on paper. Do not write in the book.

TEST 9: Social Science

STEPS TO FOLLOW
I. Read each question.
II. Choose the *best* answer.
III. Look at the answer spaces at the right or at your answer sheet.
IV. Fill in the space which has the same number as the answer you have chosen.

A Chicago is the name of a large city in
1 Mexico
2 Canada
3 United States
4 New York   A ① ② ■ ④

1 In which season would you probably see children in Chicago go swimming?
1 summer
2 spring
3 sunshine
4 daytime   1 ① ② ③ ④

2 In a hot-cold climate, the winter days are
1 long
2 not too cold
3 cold
4 rainy   2 ① ② ③ ④

3 Which one of these things was the most important to the Indians?
1 highways
2 buffalo
3 cattle
4 supermarkets   3 ① ② ③ ④

4 Lake Michigan is an important
1 natural resource
2 canal system
3 market
4 airport   4 ① ② ③ ④

5 Which one of these things will you probably see in a hot climate?
1 volcanoes
2 swimming pools
3 sleds
4 icebergs   5 ① ② ③ ④

6 When the season changes, winter is followed by
1 summer
2 July
3 December
4 spring   6 ① ② ③ ④

7 People who use natural resources wisely will
1 use one resource at a time
2 try to use them all up
3 use only the resources they need
4 never use resources   7 ① ② ③ ④

8 What do all living things need to stay alive?
1 sunshine
2 oxygen
3 algae
4 plankton   8 ① ② ③ ④

267

This test will show how well you understand social studies. Fill in the space on your answer sheet that goes with the answer you choose.

Read the story below and answer questions 1-6.

Today, most Americans live in urban areas, that is, cities and their suburbs. The chief reason for this is that there is a wider choice of jobs in urban areas.

Many things can influence where people choose to live in an urban area. Sometimes people choose to live in the suburbs because they don't like the noise and crowding of the city. Or, they think suburbs have less crime and better schools than the city.

Some people choose the city because they like all the different kinds of people and all the things there are to do there.

1 Today, most Americans live in
   1 apartments
   2 mountain areas
   3 farm areas
   4 urban areas

2 Many people choose to live in a suburb because
   1 they think it has less crime
   2 jobs are easier to find there
   3 schools are bigger in suburbs
   4 weather is better in suburbs

3 Most Americans live in urban areas because
   1 many kinds of jobs are there
   2 travel to suburbs is difficult
   3 most people work in suburbs
   4 cities are busy but not noisy

4 Which one of the following is an urban area?
   1 Illinois
   2 Lake Michigan
   3 Southeast Shopping Mall
   4 Chicago

5 Which one of the following would you *not* find in most suburbs?
   1 parking lots
   2 skyscrapers
   3 supermarkets
   4 houses

6 Another name for cities and their suburbs is
   1 suburban areas
   2 urban areas
   3 farming areas
   4 vacation areas

This test will show how well you understand social studies graphs. Fill in the space on your answer sheet that goes with the answer you choose.

Study the graph. Choose the *best* answer to questions 1 to 5.

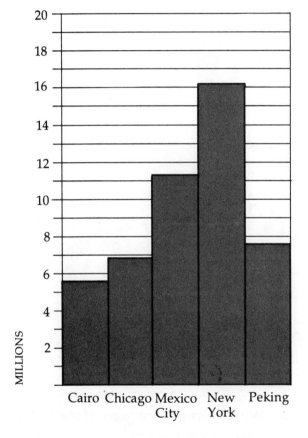

1   Which one of the following things is not shown on the graph?
1   the population of Peking
2   the population of five cities
3   the population of Cairo
4   the population of five states

2   How many cities have a larger population than Chicago?
1   one
2   two
3   three
4   four

3   How many cities have a smaller population than Chicago?
1   one
2   two
3   three
4   four

4   What do the numbers along the left-hand side of the graph stand for?
1   the size of each city
2   the city's population in millions
3   the height of each city
4   the number of city visitors

5   Which city has a population of about 7½ million?
1   Cairo
2   Peking
3   Chicago
4   New York

Level 9 Begin Here

Below is a map of Chicago. Use the map to answer the questions on this page.

This is a test of your ability to read a map. For each exercise decide which answer is correct. Then mark the proper answer space on your answer sheet. Mark only one answer space for each exercise.

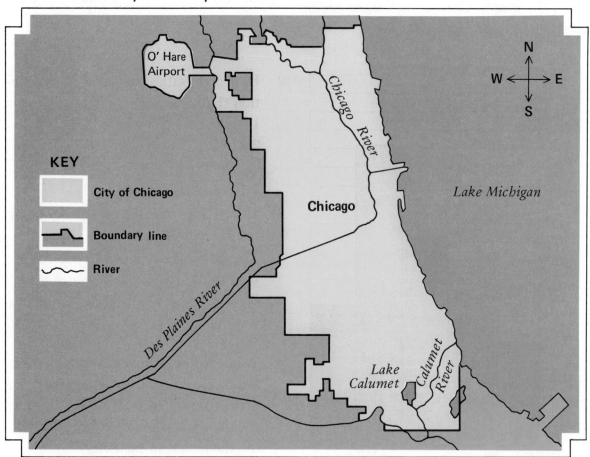

KEY

City of Chicago

Boundary line

River

1. **What does the yellow area show?**
   1) the population of Chicago
   2) the beach
   3) the shape of Chicago
   4) the airport

2. **If your plane landed at O'Hare airport, which direction would you go to reach Lake Michigan?**
   1) north   3) west
   2) south   4) east

3. **Which river forms part of the boundary of Chicago?**
   1) Michigan River
   2) O'Hare River
   3) Chicago River
   4) Des Plaines River

4. **Lake Michigan is what direction from Chicago?**
   1) west   3) north
   2) east   4) south

270

Glossary

Pronunciation key

a hat	**i** it	**oi** oil	**ch** child		a in about
ā age	**ī** ice	**ou** out	**ng** long		e in taken
ä far	**o** hot	**u** cup	**sh** she	ə =	i in pencil
e let	**ō** open	**u̇** put	**th** thin		o in lemon
ē equal	**ô** order	**ü** rule	**ŦH** then		u in circus
ėr term			**zh** measure		

amendment, (ə mend′mənt), *noun,* change.

ancient, (ān′shənt), *adjective,* belonging to times long ago.

archaeologist, (är′kē ol′ə jist), *noun,* a person who studies the things left behind by people who lived long ago.

attitude, (at′ə tüd), *noun,* way a person feels toward something.

ban, (ban), *verb,* forbid or prohibit.

belief, (bi lēf′), *noun,* an idea a person holds to be true.

boom, (büm), *noun,* rapid growth in business, building, and prices.

boundary, (boun′dərē), *noun,* something that shows the limits.

card, (kärd), *verb,* comb out or brush with a wire brush.

climate, (klī′mit), *noun,* the kind of weather a place has over many months or years.

colonist, (kol′ə nist), *noun,* a person who lives in a colony.

colony, (kol′ə nē), *noun,* a group of communities in one country that is ruled by another country.

community, (kə myü′nə tē), *noun,* all of the people living in the same place.

complex, (kəm pleks′), *adjective,* made up of a number of parts.

concentrate (kon′sən trāt), *verb,* pay close attention.

custom, (kus′təm), *noun,* habit or way of doing something that a group of people follows over a long period of time.

descendants, (di sen′dənts), *noun,* the children, grandchildren, great-grandchildren, etc., born to a certain family or group.

dweller, (dwel′ər), *noun,* a person who lives in a certain place.

employer, (em ploi′er), *noun,* person or company that gives work and pay to others.

energy, (en′ər jē), *noun,* power.

fiber, (fī′bər), *noun,* hairlike strand.

271

generation, (jen'ə rā'shən), *noun,* the people born in the same period.

government, (guv'ərn mənt), *noun,* the way a town, city, state, or country is ruled.

Great Lakes, (Grāt Lāks), *noun,* chain of five lakes, Superior, Michigan, Huron, Erie, Ontario, in central North America.

Great Plains, (Grāt Plānz), *noun,* the grasslands of central and western North America.

hide, (hīd), *noun,* an animal's skin.

immigrant, (im'ə grənt), *noun,* person who moves from one country to another.

industrial, (in dus'trē əl), *adjective,* having something to do with industry.

interdependent, (in'tər di pen'dent), *adjective,* depending on one another.

laboratory, (lab'rə tôr'ē), *noun,* place where scientific work is done.

location, (lō kā'shən), *noun,* place or position of something.

272

loom, (lüm), *noun,* frame that yarn is tied to for weaving cloth.

message, (mes'ij), *noun,* words sent from one person to another.

mood, (müd), *noun,* state of mind or feeling.

nation, (nā'shən), *noun,* country; group of people living in the same area, under the same government.

native, (nā tiv), *noun,* the place or country of birth.

natural resource, (nach'ər əl ri sôrs'), *noun,* material supplied by nature that is useful for life.

population, (pop'yə lā'shən), *noun,* the number of people.

product, (prod'əkt), *noun,* something people make or grow.

raw wool, (rô wùl), *noun,* wool just as it comes off the sheep's back.

real estate, (rē'əl e stāt), *noun,* land and buildings, property.

recreation, (rek'rē ā'shən), *noun,* fun or play.

recycle, (rē sī'kel), *verb,* treat

something so it can be used again.

refinery, (ri fī′nər ē), *noun,* factory that purifies something before it can be used.

representative, (rep′ri zen′tə tiv), *noun,* person chosen to act or speak for others.

residential, (rez′ə den′shəl), *adjective,* having something to do with homes.

resource, (ri sôrs′), *noun,* any supply that meets a need.

respond, (ri spond′), *verb,* to speak or act in answer.

rural, (rür′əl), *adjective,* in the country.

season, (sē′zn), *noun,* one of the four periods of the year; spring, summer, autumn, or winter.

sewage, (sü′ij), *noun,* the waste matter that passes through sewers.

shun, (shun), *verb,* keep away from.

shuttle, (shut′l), *noun,* device used in weaving that carries the thread back and forth across the piece being woven.

slavery, (slā′vər ē), *noun,* custom of owning people who are used as servants.

social group, (sō′shəl grüp), *noun,* people who share common goals and problems.

spindle, (spin′dl), *noun,* a rod used in spinning to twist, wind, and hold thread.

suburb, (sub′ėrb′), *noun,* town or area just outside or near a city.

succeed, (sək sēd′), *verb,* do well, have success.

system, (sis′təm), *noun,* a set of things or parts that make up a whole.

taxes, (taks′əz), *noun,* money paid by people for new roads, police protection, and so on.

urban, (ėr′ban), *adjective,* having something to do with a city.

vote, (vōt), *verb,* support a person or idea by officially making a choice.

weather, (weth′ər), *noun,* day-to-day changes in the hotness, coldness, dryness, and wetness of a place.

weave, (wēv), *verb,* twist and tie the threads of yarn together so they become one piece of cloth.

yarn, (yärn), *noun,* any spun thread.

Index

275

Acknowledgments

Quoted Material

16–21 "How Spider Got a Thin Waist" adapted from The ADVENTURES OF SPIDER by Joyce Cooper Arkhurst, by permission of Little, Brown and Co. Copyright © 1964 by Joyce Cooper Arkhurst. **27** © 1976 United Feature Syndicate, Inc. **52–53** "Bad Day" from THE WAY THINGS ARE AND OTHER POEMS by Myra Cohn Livingston (A Margaret K. McElderry Book). Copyright © 1974 by Myra Cohn Livingston. Used by permission of Atheneum Publishers and McIntosh and Otis, Inc. **76** "Two People" from THE FLATTERED FLYING FISH by E. V. Rieu, copyright © 1962 by E. V. Rieu. Published by E. P. Dutton & Com- n pany, Inc. Reprinted by permission of the author. **96–97** CHICAGO SUN-TIMES PhotOpinion, August 7, 1977 by Sharon Kornegay. CHICAGO SUN-TIMES photos by Carmen Reporto. Reprinted with permission of The Chicago Sun-Times. **104** "Understanding." From THE MOON AND A STAR. © 1965 by Myra Cohn Livingston. Reprinted by permission of Harcourt Brace Jovanovich, Inc. **155** "Downtown" from TOWN AND COUNTRYSIDE POEMS by John Travers Moore © 1968 by John Travers Moore. Used with the permission of Albert Whitman & Company. **159–161** Adapted from "Blacks renewing ghetto 'roots' . . ." by Clarence Page, CHICAGO TRIBUNE, March 6, 1977. Reprinted, courtesy of the Chicago Tribune. **166** "From Sheep to Cloth" by Marian Payne. Adapted from the March issue of TEACHER Magazine with permission of the publisher. This article is copyrighted. © 1978 by Macmillan Professional Magazines, Inc. All rights reserved. **198** "List of Privileges" from pamphlet published in London, 1667. Cited in THE AMERICAN PEOPLE by Bernard A. Weisberger. Published by American Heritage Publishing Co., Inc., 1970, 1971. **206–207** "Letter to Mother Elsa" from Kerstin. Reprinted by permission of Karstin Olofsson. Copyright © 1979 Scott, Foresman and Company. **210, 212** From "That World We Call Chinatown" by Robert Cross, CHICAGO TRIBUNE MAGAZINE, Feb. 5, 1978. Reprinted, courtesy of the Chicago Tribune. **242–244** Abridgment of "Happy Bee" from RANGER RICK'S NATURE MAGAZINE, October 1976. Reprinted by permission of the publisher, the National Wildlife Federation.

Illustrations

Cover Friendship, Dir. by James Yanagisawa and Santi Isrowuthakul, 1973, Haines Public School, 247 West 23rd Place, Chicago, Ill., photo by John Weber. **3, 5** (parrot, rabbit) Leonard Lee Rue III/VAN CLEVE PHOTOGRAPHY. **72–3** Walter Iooss, Jr./SPORTS ILLUSTRATED © 1978 Time Inc. **78–9** Robert Amft. **82–5** John Launois/BLACK STAR. **86** Thomas Putney/DELAWARE PHOTO LIBRARY INC. **87** Kenneth B. Maatman. **88, 89, 92** (bottom) John Launois/BLACK STAR. **94–5** John R. Bayalis/VINCENT J. KAMIN & ASSOCIATES. **96–7** James P. Rowan. **98–9** Gianni Tortoli/PHOTO RESEARCHERS INC. **100** Omar Marcus/VAN CLEVE PHOTOGRAPHY. **104–5** Peter Menzel/STOCK, BOSTON. **106** Harrison Forman. **108–9** Courtesy of the National Park Service, Catoctin Mountain Park. **110** Alfred B. Thomas/EARTH SCENES. **111** Dale Wittner. **112–3** Carlton McAvey. **114–5** W. B. Finch/STOCK, BOSTON. **116–7** Courtesy of National Collection of Fine Arts, Smithsonian Institution. **120–1** Bill Benoit. **122–3** Dan Guravich/PHOTO RESEARCHERS INC. **124–5** Rapho Division/PHOTO RESEARCHERS INC. **124** (inset) Dale Wittner. **125** (inset) C. C. Lockwood/EARTH SCENES. **126** Frederick Myers/VAN CLEVE PHOTOGRAPHY **128–9** Dale Wittner. **132–3** Wm. Franklin McMahon. **145** SHOSTAL ASSOCIATES INC. **146** Erich Hartmann/MAGNUM PHOTOS. **148–153** Photographs, Arlette Mellaart. **154–5** Robert Amft. **156–7** (center left) C. Vergara/PHOTO RESEARCHERS INC. (center right) Tom McHugh/PHOTO RESEARCHERS INC. (right) Charles Harbutt/MAGNUM PHOTOS. **167** (bottom) Gerry Souter/VAN CLEVE PHOTOGRAPHY. **176** (top) Courtesy of Wellman Industries Inc. (center) Burns/FPG PHOTO ASSOCIATES. (bottom) Pastner/FPG PHOTO ASSOCIATES. **182–3** Robert Amft. **189** Detail from a mural by James Eli Bowden. **190** Detail from a mural by James Eli Bowden. **192** Detail from a mural by James Eli Bowden. **194** Courtesy of the American Antiquarian Society. **195** Courtesy of the Trustees of the British Museum. **198** Rare Book Division, The New York Public Library, Astor, Lenox and Tilden Foundations. **201** The National Maritime Museum, London. **204** Photoworld/FPG PHOTO ASSOCIATES. **205** Jean-Claude Lejeune. **206** Robert Amft. **208–9** Barbara Van Cleve/VAN CLEVE PHOTOGRAPHY. **211** Brown Brothers. **212** Burk Uzzle/MAGNUM PHOTOS. **215** George Holton/PHOTO RESEARCHERS INC. **216** Thailand Today, courtesy Time-Life Books Inc. **217** Van Bucher/PHOTO RESEARCHERS INC. **220** Pictorial Parade, Inc. **240–1** FPG PHOTO ASSOCIATES.